British History in Perspective
General Editor: Jeremy Black

PUBLISHED TITLES

Please see overleaf for forthcoming titles

FORTHCOMING TITLES

POLITICAL LIFE IN MEDIEVAL ENGLAND, 1300–1450

W. M. ORMROD

St. Martin's Press

First published in Great Britain 1995 by
MACMILLAN PRESS LTD
Houndmills, Basingstoke, Hampshire RG21 6XS
and London
Companies and representatives
throughout the world

A catalogue record for this book is available
from the British Library.

ISBN 0–333–59243–3 hardcover
ISBN 0–333–59244–1 paperback

10   9   8   7   6   5   4   3   2   1
04   03   02   01   00   99   98   97   96   95

Printed in Malaysia

First published in the United States of America 1995 by
Scholarly and Reference Division,
ST. MARTIN'S PRESS, INC.,
175 Fifth Avenue,
New York, N.Y. 10010

ISBN 0–312–12722–7

Library of Congress Cataloging-in-Publication Data
Ormrod, W. M., 1957–
Political life in medieval England, 1300–1450 / W. M. Ormrod.
p. cm. — (British history in perspective)
Includes bibliographical references and index.
ISBN 0–312–12722–7
1. Great Britain—Politics and government—1066–1485. 2. Great
Britain—History—House of Lancaster, 1399–1461. 3. England—Social
life and customs—1066–1485. 4. Great Britain—History—14th
century. I. Title. II. Series.
DA225.O76 1995
941.03'7—dc20   95–8258
                                                         CIP

CONTENTS

PREFACE

This book is intended as an exploration of the dimensions and concerns of political society in England during the period of the 'long' Hundred Years War. Although it draws extensively on the researches and ideas of many historians currently working in this field (and to whom apologies are immediately necessary for the brevity and therefore the inadequacy of citations), it aims not simply to synthesise and reconcile but also to provide a personal interpretation of a subject that now, more than ever, excites diverse and sometimes conflicting conclusions. My principal debt of gratitude is to my undergraduate and graduate students at the University of York, whose liveliness and intelligence has been a constant inspiration for the last few years. More immediately, Valery Rose and Maggie Jones have helped guide my text through the press. Finally, Sarah provided the space and time that I so urgently needed to complete the project; to her, my special thanks.

August 1994   W. M. Ormrod

GLOSSARY

banneret   A military and social rank denoting knighthood but superior to that of ordinary knight; a banneret was entitled to carry a square banner as distinct from the knight's pennon.

chamber   The king's private quarters and the household department responsible for administering them.

chancery   The principal secretarial office of the English state; its senior officer, the chancellor, was the keeper of the great seal.

chevauchée   From the French *chevaucher*, to ride; an extended raid through enemy territory.

common pleas   The central common law court with jurisdiction over civil pleas; sat almost always at Westminster.

demesne   Land held by a lord or the king in person and not let out to farm.

escheat   Land and other rights reverting to a feudal lord on the death of a vassal.

exchequer   The main financial department of the state, presided over by the treasurer.

eyre   A judicial circuit; from the Latin *iter*, a journey.

hundred   Administrative sub-division of a shire (called a wapentake in certain parts of the country).

indenture   Contract written up in duplicate form and then cut along a jagged or 'indented' line, thus allowing each party to keep a copy of the agreement.

king's bench The superior common law court having criminal jurisdiction, sitting normally at Westminster but sometimes patrolling the provinces.

lollards Followers of the teachings of John Wyclif, the late fourteenth-century Oxford theologian who denied the authority of the papacy and questioned the Catholic doctrine of transubstantiation.

privy seal Formerly the king's personal seal, though from the mid-fourteenth century a department of state and the main secretariat of the royal council.

signet The king's personal or 'secret' seal, held in the custody of his secretary.

vill Village or township; an administrative unit distinct from the manor (the feudal unit) and the parish (the ecclesiastical unit).

wardrobe The main financial department of the royal household.

1

POLITICAL SOCIETY AND POLITICAL EVENTS

Did politics matter in later medieval England? The answer depends largely on how we define our terms. If politics means participation in public life and direct involvement in the making and implementation of policy, then presumably not. If, however, we think of the 'political life' in the title of this book more in terms of 'political consciousness' – that is, an awareness of the personalities, events, institutions and policies that determined the way the kingdom was run, then our perception of the parameters of politics is transformed. Late medieval England was one of the most highly organised and unified realms in Europe: indeed, the early development of a local royal administration and a centralised royal bureaucracy, the extraordinary uniformity of judicial and fiscal structures, the remarkable extension of royal authority over the church and the emergence of parliament, a single assembly, representative (in theory) of the entire kingdom, make this one of the very few later medieval kingdoms that genuinely deserve to be called 'states'.[1] Much of the process of state-building had in fact been completed by the early fourteenth century, and the later Middle Ages, although witnessing some further important extensions in the scope of royal governance, is usually characterised as the period in which the political community began to come to terms with – and sometimes kick against – the new authority claimed by the crown. The major task facing the historian of what might, for present purposes, be called the 'political culture' of the late Middle Ages is therefore to assess the number and status of those whose lives were touched by the state, and the way in which they responded to that experience. That is the primary purpose of this book.

Political Society

The twelfth and thirteenth centuries had witnessed a sustained and, by medieval standards, a dramatic growth in both the population and the economy of England. The increase in the birth rate may, however, have proceeded faster than the increase in agricultural productivity, and some historians believe that by 1300 there was a dangerous imbalance between the population and the resources needed to support it. The dramatic reports of distress and mortality during the disastrous famines of 1316–17 and 1321–22 certainly suggest that the population had become even more vulnerable than usual to the vagaries of the harvest. Little more than a generation later, the country was hit by the greatest human tragedy ever experienced in the British Isles. Such was the virulence of the Black Death of 1348–9 and the series of plagues that followed it that by the 1370s the human population had been reduced to between a half and two-thirds of its former size, and for most of the following century English society numbered a mere 2 million to 3 million people.

The Black Death not only restored the balance between population and resources, it also changed the way that wealth was distributed through society. In the thirteenth century, high demand for food, high prices in the marketplace and an abundant supply of labour had given the advantage to landholders, encouraging them to manage their estates directly and live off the profits of the land. By the end of the fourteenth century, with grain prices falling, customary services increasingly difficult to enforce and the costs of wage labour rising, the majority of the great aristocratic and ecclesiastical landholders came to realise that their only sensible option lay in leasing their demesnes. Consequently, a large amount of new land became available for members of the gentry and the peasantry. While the nobility and the greater ecclesiastical landholders were very far from being impoverished, this process, coupled with the striking increase in the earning capacity and purchasing power of wage labourers, undoubtedly created a major improvement in the living standards, and by extension the relative social status, of a substantial proportion of the rural population.[2]

The first point to make about the political culture of late medieval England is that it therefore operated in a social and economic context that differed in important respects not just from what came later but also from what had gone before. This was an extraordinarily small world. The parliamentary lords temporal, who increasingly reserved to themselves the special status of a 'nobility', numbered between 50 and 100 men; the intermarriages between their own families and (increasingly in this period) the royal dynasty created a particularly intricate web of political relationships. The recruitment of members of the high aristocracy into the episcopate, which is such a feature of the later fourteenth and fifteenth centuries, further enhanced the sense of solidarity among the landed elite. The groups of lesser landholders who were denied 'nobility' but aspired to 'gentility' may have been considerably larger in total numbers (perhaps 4,000 families by the end of our period),[3] but were, at least at the local level, just as tightly interconnected. The emergence by the fifteenth century of a three-fold hierarchy within the gentry – knights, esquires, and gentlemen – was itself in part a reflection of the desire constantly to refine and redefine the smaller networks created within this larger social group.

This small world was not, however, an altogether exclusive one. The later fourteenth and particularly the fifteenth century witnessed the emergence of an increasingly complex and flexible social hierarchy. Unlike most other parts of medieval Europe, England did not follow the convention of bestowing particular privileges on social groups: except for the notion of peerage, which, from the early fourteenth century, gave the parliamentary lords the right to trial before their equals, the upper orders of English society enjoyed no particular judicial or fiscal privileges. Consequently, while *nobility* depended on the grant of a title from the king, *gentility* was largely self-defining.[4] The increase in the number of men using the titles of esquire and gentleman during the fifteenth century is to be explained not simply in terms of a growing self-consciousness among the existing landed classes but also by the growing popularity of such labels among other sections of society. To the extent that the achievement of gentility also guaranteed political status, the background and influence of these 'new' gentry is worth some consideration. Two groups are of particular significance in this respect: merchants and lawyers.

Partly as a result of the constitutional position of some towns as self-governing corporations and partly because of the growing importance of overseas trade in the economy of the realm, merchants were increasingly drawn into the world of royal government and high politics from the late thirteenth century.[5] The importance of the merchant class to the successful functioning of the state was particularly emphasised when the financial demands of the Hundred Years War drove the crown to seek new sources of credit. The promotion of the first of a new breed of English bankers, William de la Pole, into the ranks of the gentry, and of his son Michael into the very highest ranks of the peerage, may have been unique in the later Middle Ages, but it highlights a much more general trend. From the mid-fourteenth century an increasing number of London merchants and financiers received knighthood from the crown. And when the Statute of Additions of 1413 required those cited in legal documents to be described by profession or status, many leading merchants both in the capital and in provincial towns preferred to identify themselves not according to their misteries but by the titles of esquire and gentleman. The political integration of the merchant class clearly depended a good deal on the assumption of the values, as well as the status, of gentility.

The emergence of professional lawyers as a recognisable element in political society itself owed much to the development of the state and the expansion of royal justice during the twelfth and thirteenth centuries.[6] By the early fourteenth century, lucrative careers were being made not only by the elite corps of serjeants at law and others qualified to plead in the central courts but also by a much larger group of men – to be numbered literally in thousands –

who provided a wide range of professional services in their own localities, from drafting legal documents to acting as attorneys (that is, official representatives) in cases brought before the king's judges. The laicisation of royal and aristocratic bureaucracies during the later fourteenth and fifteenth centuries also allowed them many opportunities to develop careers in administration. In a society that increasingly recognised function and wealth alongside the possession of land as a legitimate qualification for political participation, the professional lawyer began to establish a remarkably prominent place in public life. The parallels with the merchants are striking: provincial lawyers assumed the rank of gentleman; royal lawyers promoted to the bench received knighthood; many legal dynasties intermarried with the landed elite and became assimilated into the gentry; and a few – such as the Scropes of Bolton and Masham in the fourteenth century and the Bourchiers in the fifteenth – worked their way into the ranks of the peerage. To contemporaries, the upwardly mobile lawyer was more frequently a focus of suspicion and resentment than a cause for celebration, but to the historian he encapsulates much about the growing complexity and diversity of the late medieval polity.

The most striking example of the increasing heterogeneity of political society in the century after the Black Death, however, is provided by the top ranks of peasant society.[7] In the sliding scale of payments established for a royal poll tax in 1379, 'serjeants', 'franklins' and 'farmers of manors and parsonages' were distinguished from the rest of the rural population and required to pay between 1s. and 6s. 8d. as against the standard 4d. demanded from the majority of the peasantry.[8] A number of these social groups would, in the succeeding generations, be absorbed into the emerging and expanding class of gentlemen. But the standard terminology developed in the fifteenth century to distinguish the ranks of the rural population – yeoman, husbandman, labourer and servant – also indicated the existence of a substantial peasant elite that was not accepted as 'gentle' and yet still had sufficient economic and legal status to allow it some degree of participation in public affairs. The political status of the yeoman particularly calls out for fuller analysis. A yeoman was usually a freeholder with 60 acres or more. He farmed the land himself (his willingness to undertake manual work was what ultimately prevented him from claiming gentility) but he also employed lesser peasants as agricultural labourers and household servants. He produced not just for subsistence but for the market, and his income, though typically under £10 (the figure that contemporaries took to be sufficient to maintain a gentleman), might also be considerably higher. In 1436 there were at least 3,500 men whose annual income from land was between £5 and £10, and although a proportion of this group represented the bottom end of the squirearchy, there is little doubt that a large number of such men would have been identified by contemporaries as yeomen.[9] If the group could be extended to include those with incomes from freeholds in excess of £2 a year (the figure that came increasingly in the fifteenth century to be seen as the cut-off point for participation in public life), it would be clear that the yeomanry comprised the largest class so far identified as candidates for inclusion in the late medieval political community. Despite the obvious overlap, and the frequent passage, between the ranks of yeoman and gentleman, the most interesting thing about this peasant elite is that, unlike the merchants and lawyers discussed above, it did not need the credibility conferred by gentility to qualify it for participation in the lower reaches of government and politics. If we are to count the yeomanry as part of the political society that emerged in England during the century after the Black Death, then we have to recognise not only the growing proportion of the population that made up the polity but also, and perhaps more importantly, the diversity of experience and circumstance contained within it.

So far, we have been attempting to characterise political society in terms of those groups that could claim direct representation in, or some direct influence over, the course of public affairs. The institutions and channels through which such classes controlled the making and implementation of policy are discussed in chapters 2–3. For the present, however, it must be stressed that the 'political life' to which the title of this book refers was by no means the monopoly even of this expanding power elite. Direct participation in politics may have been a minority activity, but there was no monopoly on political consciousness. One of the most interesting developments of the fourteenth and fifteenth centuries was the emergence of what would now be called public opinion, not merely among the elite but in a wide cross-section of the population. The simultaneous decline of seigneurial authority and growth of royal government during the fourteenth and fifteenth centuries had the effect of bringing the crown – represented in real terms by tax assessors and judicial commissioners – into much more direct and regular contact with town and village communities. Just as the proprietary classes had been forced to come to terms with the intrusions of the Angevin regime in the twelfth and thirteenth centuries, so now the mass of the peasantry was, for the first time, confronted with the immediate and often controversial presence of the state. The Ordinance and Statute of Labourers, imposed by the crown and the proprietary classes in the immediate aftermath of the Black Death in a vain attempt to put back the clock and maintain agricultural and other wages at their pre-plague levels, provided the most striking – not to say disturbing – example of this intrusive new force. If the most obvious popular responses to such developments are to be found in the uprisings and protest literature of the period, there are also, as we shall see, many other more subtle ways in which the peasantry, or certain groups within it, can be seen to have become reconciled with the system of public authority that emerged in the 150 years covered by this study.[10]

'Political life' therefore encompasses a great deal more than the long series of events that shaped the fortunes of the monarchy, and provides the stock in trade of standard political histories of this period. However, this book is also predicated on the notion that England was a single political unit bound together by administrative and cultural traditions in which events at the centre remained relevant to those groups that controlled government and formed public opinion in the localities. Before proceeding to a study of the institutions and issues that engaged this polity, it is therefore important and relevant to understand the context of events in which the political culture of late medieval England was formed.

Political Events

During the first half of his reign, Edward I had pursued an ambitious policy of legal and administrative reform designed to re-establish the monarchy after the débâcle of Henry III's civil wars. From the 1290s, however, governmental priorities changed as military enterprises – against France from 1294 to 1298 and against Scotland from 1296 to the end of the reign and beyond – dominated the political agenda. The intense fiscal burdens imposed on the country to support the war for the recovery of Gascony created deep discontent, and in 1297 a group of barons, led by the earls of Hereford and Norfolk, refused to co-operate in the mustering of an army for service in France and threatened armed resistance against the crown. Edward was reluctantly persuaded to step down and issue the Confirmation of the Charters, which restricted prerogative levies and guaranteed that the king would seek consent for general taxes. But despite further concessions made in the Articles upon the Charters in 1300, it became obvious that formal compromises won at moments of political crisis counted for little when set against the realities of everyday government. Edward fell back increasingly on loans and on his feudal resources as a means of financing the continued military commitment in Scotland and gradually extricated himself from the already rather empty promises made in 1297 and 1300. The extent to which this demonstration of bad faith created a permanent resentment against Edward I and influenced the opposition to his successor is still uncertain, but the opening decade of the fourteenth century certainly offered little expectation of a notable revival in the popularity of the Plantagenet regime.

If Edward II was unlucky in his inheritance, there can be little doubt that his own personality provided the real key to the general unease and frequent political conflicts of his reign. Edward's friendship with the Gascon knight Piers Gaveston was already public knowledge at court before the accession, and Gaveston's blatant upstaging of the young Queen Isabella during the coronation of 1308 left no one among the nobility in any doubt as to the political implications. Concern stemmed not simply from the possibility that the two men were engaged in a homosexual relationship (an assumption that has, in any case, recently been challenged) but from the king's stubborn determination to promote Gaveston to the very highest levels of the English aristocracy and give him substantial control over the direction of policy.[11] The resulting antagonisms provided the background to the New Ordinances of 1311, in which the baronage demanded the permanent exile of the king's friend. Edward II's long struggle with his cousin Thomas of Lancaster, though ostensibly concerned with the implementation of the Ordinances, would probably never have reached such intensity had it not been for the personal animosities aroused by the attack on, and subsequent murder of, Gaveston in 1311–12. The emergence of a new favourite, Hugh Despenser, in the early 1320s was therefore sufficiently threatening that Lancaster and his allies were prepared to take up arms in open rebellion against the king.

The unexpected victory of the royal party at the battle of Boroughbridge in 1322 brought down Lancaster and his followers, who were subjected to summary trial, loss of titles and estates and punishment by imprisonment or death. The impact of this episode, and the hatred engendered by the subsequent Despenser regime, is most strikingly revealed by the actions of one of Lancaster's erstwhile supporters, Roger Mortimer of Wigmore. Escaping from the Tower of London, Mortimer fled to France where he was able to establish contact with the disaffected queen and persuade her to use her young son, whom she had taken to France to perform homage for Aquitaine in 1325, as a means of challenging the English throne. The active and passive support given to their invasion in September 1326 was striking proof of the widespread contempt in which Edward II was now held, and his capture and forced resignation of the throne were effected not only with remarkable speed but also with surprisingly little bloodshed. The intense relief felt at the departure of Edward II seems to have been sufficient to overcome any qualms about the constitutional validity of the deposition and encourage hopes of a swift return to a more conventional and amenable style of monarchy.

It took some time to demonstrate the point clearly, but the regime of Edward III did indeed fulfil that model of medieval kingship. Although the minority administration made humiliating agreements with the French in 1327 and the Scots in 1328, Edward was quick to identify himself with the martial traditions of his grandfather's reign and to make war first in the north and then, after 1337, across the Channel. In 1340 he laid claim to the throne of France by right of descent through his mother, the sister of the last ruler of the house of Capet. Whether Edward actually believed in this claim we shall never know, but most historians have seen it merely as a diplomatic posture designed to bring pressure to bear on the Valois monarchy and secure the essential concession that had evaded both of Edward's immediate predecessors: namely, release from the terms of the treaty of Paris of 1259 and full sovereign control over the duchy of Aquitaine. Edward's strategy in the late 1330s did little to inspire confidence at home, and in 1340–1 there was a serious rift between the king and the domestic council. However, the resulting political crisis seems to have focused not on the making of war itself but simply on its administration, and does not therefore compare with the threat of baronial insurrection encountered by Edward I in 1297, let alone the realities of armed rebellion faced by every other king in the period covered by this book. To an extent, the consensus that characterised domestic politics in the middle years of the fourteenth century clearly owed itself to the notable series of victories – Neville's Cross (1346), Crécy (1346), Calais (1347) and Poitiers (1356) – won by Edward and his commanders. On the other hand, the support of the English political community could only be secured through carefully timed and skilfully judged concessions. By limiting certain of his prerogative powers, acknowledging the commons' control over taxation and recognising the particular authority of legislation made in parliament, Edward was able to exploit the financial resources of the realm to a greater extent than any of his predecessors. By 1360, with a highly advantageous settlement to the Anglo-French dispute apparently within his grasp, Edward III seemed set for the sort of historical reputation enjoyed in his own time by Henry II and in later centuries by Henry V.

That reputation was inevitably tarnished by the failure of the peace proposals, the renewal of the French war and the king's gradual descent into feeble old age. The 1370s proved to be one of the most dismal decades in the political history of later medieval

England, as military reversals abroad combined with financial ineptitude, political faction and court scandals at home to generate antagonism among both the governing classes and the wider population. In 1376 the commons in parliament framed a series of accusations against members of the royal household and their associates, thereby happening upon the process known as impeachment. Even though the crown was quick to reverse the judgments once the crisis was passed, the so-called Good Parliament had set important precedents for future political opposition to the crown. The succession of the boy-king Richard II in 1377 offered no real hope of remission and in a sense made the crown still more vulnerable to both political and popular criticism: those who marched on London during the Peasants' Revolt of 1381 may well have found it easier to challenge a group of ministers perceived to be abusing the extraordinary power vested in them during the minority than to face an adult king fully responsible for his own regime.

Not that Richard's gradual emergence into active politics in the 1380s proved to have a calming effect. Indeed, it was precisely in those areas where the king was perceived to have most personal influence – the disposition of patronage and the management of the royal household – that the Ricardian administration came under most criticism. In 1386 the commons repeated the procedures of the Good Parliament and impeached the king's friend and recently dismissed chancellor, Michael de la Pole, earl of Suffolk. This was followed by the appointment of an extraordinary commission of prelates and nobles empowered to make far-reaching inquiries into the king's finances and to undertake the general management of the household. Richard's hostility to this major infringement of his prerogative arguably coloured his actions throughout the rest of his life. Certainly, the continued suspicion of the king's friends, provoking armed insurrection in 1387 and a series of highly dubious trials in the parliament of 1388, made a complete reconciliation with the baronial opposition highly unlikely. Whether Richard was deliberately pursuing a policy of appeasement in the early 1390s or merely biding his time and waiting for the opportunity to attack his opponents remains a matter of debate. But whatever the case, the arrests of the earls of

Arundel and Warwick and of the king's own uncle, Thomas of Woodstock, duke of Gloucester, in 1397, looked suspiciously like the first stage in a calculated plan to eliminate the great lords who had contrived to limit the king's power in 1386–8. That process was completed by the sentences of exile pronounced against Thomas Mowbray, duke of Norfolk, and Richard's cousin, Henry of Bolingbroke, duke of Hereford, in 1398, and by the king's subsequent refusal to allow Bolingbroke to inherit the duchy of Lancaster on the death of John of Gaunt in 1399. Through Richard's own political ineptitude and Hereford's equally unscrupulous opportunism, the latter's invasion, launched for the purpose of claiming his rightful inheritance, turned into a much more dubious bid for the throne and Bolingbroke found himself installed as king of England in September 1399.

There was much more to Richard II's tyranny than the vendetta against his baronial opponents: by extracting forced loans, by extorting novel oaths of obedience, and by cajoling some of his subjects to accept that the crown had *carte blanche* over their property, Richard had breached the trust invested in the monarchy and offended a wide cross-section of the political community.[12] The new king, not surprisingly, adopted a populist approach, showing considerable restraint in the punishment of Richard's supporters and promising (rashly, as it turned out) to 'live of his own'. During the early years of his reign, however, Henry IV was to face frequent threats of rebellion, first from the Ricardian nobility and then from his own erstwhile supporters, led by the earl of Northumberland. The major revolt that broke out in Wales in 1399 was an uncomfortable reminder of the tenuous nature of the Plantagenet regime within the principality; when the Welsh leader, Owain Glyndŵr, entered into an alliance with the Percys with the declared intention of putting another of Richard II's cousins, the young earl of March, on the throne, the Lancastrian regime seemed destined for rapid extinction. That Henry IV reacted quickly and firmly to these rebellions, emerged as the victor and secured the undisputed succession of his eldest son to the throne in 1413 are rightly regarded as major achievements. Yet the political legacy of Richard II's reign was also enduring, and Henry V himself had to face armed uprisings and threats of deposition not only from a group of religious extremists known as lollards in 1413–14 but also, more seriously, from within the ranks of the royal family and high aristocracy on the very eve of the great invasion of France in 1415. The very frequency of the armed rebellions against the early Lancastrian regime strongly suggests that the deposition of 1399 had created an altogether different political climate from that of 1327.

If these considerations did indeed bear on Henry V when he took up the government of the realm, it is certainly easy to explain why his reign witnessed the revival of the martial exploits that had done so much to enhance Edward III's reputation. In fact, Henry IV had already more or less committed the country to breaking Richard II's truce and reviving war with France, and it would seem that Henry V initially set out merely to continue his father's policy: namely, the recovery of the English possessions in Aquitaine offered to Edward III under the terms of the treaty of Brétigny in 1360. But the extraordinary success of the Agincourt expedition of 1415 and the lengthy Normandy campaign of 1417–19 encouraged the king to push his demands further, and by the treaty of Troyes (1420), and his resulting marriage to Charles VI's daughter, Henry was declared the rightful heir to the throne of France. In the event, Henry's premature death, followed quickly by the demise of his father-in-law, left the infant Henry VI as titular king of England and France in 1422 and threw onto the shoulders of the royal family and high nobility the awesome responsibility for establishing the Plantagenet regime across the Channel. It seems, then, that Henry V's remarkable ability to withstand the ruthless critical analysis applied by modern his- torians depends very largely on the brevity of his life and reign. This is not to deny that he was a remarkable man. But the very achievements which did so much to validate the Lancastrian regime in the eyes of contemporaries also created false hopes and artificially inflated expectations which no successor – let alone the blatantly deficient Henry VI – could ever adequately have fulfilled.

The deeds of Henry V may have cast a long shadow over the minority of his son, but they also helped to create a sense of unity and purpose within the political elite. Despite the personal rivalry between Henry VI's uncle, the duke of Gloucester, and his cousin

Henry Beaufort, bishop of Winchester, the regency councils operating between 1422 and 1437 seem to have worked sufficiently productively to be perceived as a viable form of government. In particular, the absence of any further significant armed revolts at a time when, in all other respects, the regime was at its most vulnerable emphasises the great change that Henry V had brought about in attitudes towards the Lancastrian monarchy (the lollard rising of 1431, though generating renewed concern about the revolutionary implications of heresy, was significant mainly in the way that it enhanced the reputation of its repressor, the duke of Gloucester).[13] The continued success of the English forces operating in France until 1429 also speaks much for the ability of the regency administrations in England and France. This is not to say that all was still well in 1437. But it was only when the king reached his majority and started negotiations to extricate himself from what seemed to him an unwinnable war that disaster really set in. The very act of negotiation was a tacit admission of the failure of the dual monarchy, for when Henry VI agreed to marry Margaret of Anjou, the niece of Charles VII, in 1444, he effectively recognised the legitimacy of Charles's own title to the French throne. Much more seriously, in 1445 Henry secretly promised to surrender the valuable county of Maine in return for a settlement. In the end, the negotiations simply allowed Charles VII the opportunity he needed to muster his resources for a final assault: between 1449 and 1453 the remaining English possessions in Normandy and Gascony were overrun and the war was concluded in the most decisive manner possible by the virtual elimination of English forces from France.

Meanwhile, the domestic political situation was also becoming critical. There is some debate as to whether Henry VI was actively responsible for the political problems of his regime or whether he was the instrument of others' ambitions: the psychological disorders that were to overcome him in the 1450s have naturally raised doubts as to whether he was ever much more than a titular monarch. Whatever the case, it was inevitably upon the king that much of the blame fell. Henry's unpopularity rested not merely in the collapse of Lancastrian France but also in the blatant squandering of royal resources on a new group of king's friends: in particular, the emergence of another royal favourite, William de la Pole, duke of Suffolk, during the 1440s, created intense antagonism among the high nobility and raised the spectre of revolt. The death, under highly suspicious circumstances, of Henry V's last surviving brother, Humphrey of Gloucester, in 1447 created serious concerns over the Lancastrian succession (Henry VI's only child, Edward, was not born until 1453) and gave an added dimension to the political pretensions of the king's distant cousin, Richard, duke of York. Early in 1450 Suffolk was impeached, a procedure which, given its rarity, may have been consciously modelled on the trial of his grandfather in 1386. The king's efforts to save his friend caused much ill will and a series of revolts broke out in southern England. The popular support demonstrated for Richard of York by the Kentish rebels who participated in Cade's Rebellion indicates the degree of disillusionment that Henry VI's regime had bred not only among the high nobility but also in provincial society. If the threat of open civil war was still some way off, it is not difficult, at least in hindsight, to trace the origins of the Wars of the Roses to the years immediately around 1450.

This brief outline of events may appear to give general credence to the long-standing historical convention that the years 1300–1450 marked a period of decline, crisis and eventual collapse in the political life of England. The centralised, unitary state which supposedly emerged during the thirteenth century and reached its high point in the first half of Edward I's reign was fatally compromised not simply by the personal inadequacies of Edward II, Richard II and Henry VI but also by the over-ambitious and ultimately ruinous foreign policies of Edward I, Edward III and Henry V. The result was a shift of power away from the monarchy, a new emphasis on the obligations of kingship and a belief that the dynastic principle itself applied only so long as the crown rested on a head large enough to sustain its great weight.[14]

Thus far, the conventional interpretation is neither contested nor, indeed, particularly controversial. But underpinning much of this tradition is a particular scale of values imposed by English historians in the late nineteenth century which seems increasingly at variance with the modern understanding of medieval politics. William Stubbs and his pupils saw the attainment of the sovereign state as the desirable goal – even the natural destiny – of the medieval English monarchy and represented any deviation from that path – let alone such an irresponsible deviation as the Hundred Years War – as deeply damaging not only to the authority of the crown but to the welfare of the people.[15] Consequently, it is all too easy to interpret the shift of power in the fourteenth and first half of the fifteenth centuries as a regressive and disruptive development and to see it both as the essential explanation for the Wars of the Roses and the primary justification for the subsequent restoration of central authority under the Tudors.

If, however, we take the line advocated by the late K. B. McFarlane and his successors and move from a king-centred to a polity-centred history, then our perception of the late medieval state may be significantly different.[16] To contemporaries, the wars against Scotland and France provided the most obvious form of state-building – through territorial aggrandisement – and were indeed a good deal more acceptable than the continued extension of royal authority within the realm of England. Meanwhile, the accommodation reached between the monarchy and its subjects, and particularly the integration of the gentry into public service as local agents of the crown, significantly increased the range and capacity of the state and created the kind of consensus government that was ultimately the only guarantee of social and political stability. The redistribution of power away from the monarchy and towards the nobility and gentry may therefore have given the late medieval polity a particular character, but could not in itself have accounted for the descent into civil war in the 1450s.

The purpose of this book, then, is not to establish whether the constitution of the later medieval kingdom of England was 'good' or 'bad' by nineteenth-century – or even late twentieth-century – standards, but to assess how contemporary political society both influenced and responded to important changes in the character and purpose of governance. In order to do this, we need first to understand the structures in which the polity operated and through which its concerns were communicated to the crown. We may then proceed to discuss some of the major issues that dominated political debate in this period and had such a formative influence on public opinion. In the next two chapters, which discuss the political institutions and identities of later medieval England, we shall proceed not, as is now fashionable, from the bottom up, but from the top down. The intention is not to deny that each locality had its own political society and political preoccupations but to demonstrate the degree to which the concerns of the regions were communicated through central institutions and the extent to which these structures promoted a sense of common identity in the political life of the realm.

2

POLITICAL INSTITUTIONS: THE CENTRE

Several earlier generations of historians believed that the politics of the later Middle Ages was conditioned by an innate tension between the interests of the crown and those of the baronage. They were thus able to create a coherent story of constitutional development focusing on the great political set pieces – above all, of course, the series of royal depositions – of the fourteenth and fifteenth centuries. Furthermore, they located many of the causes and preoccupations of such disputes in the developing administrative apparatus of the state. In particular, J. Conway Davies and T. F. Tout argued that there was a fundamental conflict between the agencies of the royal prerogative represented by the privy seal and wardrobe and the supposedly independent and even pro-baronial offices of state, the chancery and exchequer. For these historians, political history became, quite simply, administrative history.

This interpretation has been decisively rejected by recent scholarship, which now tends to see the various parts of the governmental machine at Westminster as forming a single and normally coherent whole devoted to maintaining the interests of the crown.[1] Partly because of this new approach, there has been a tendency of late to turn away from the centre and towards regional and local collectivities in the search for the true heart of late medieval political life. However, it has also to be stressed that there remained certain other central institutions whose functions may indeed be described as primarily political and which, furthermore, had a formative influence on the character and the agenda of politics. This chapter concentrates on the three most important such assemblies: the court, the council, and parliament.

The Court

The recognised centre of high politics in medieval England was the court. The *familia* (a word that denoted both the family and the household) was widely regarded as the most natural and powerful form of human association, and medieval noblemen in particular found it easy to identify with – and criticise – the royal court since it was only really a grander version of their own domestic establishments.[2] In analysing the political function and complexion of the later medieval court, it is necessary to recognise that this body consisted of a number of distinct groupings. For present purposes, it is helpful to define three: 'employees', the permanent staff of the household; 'retainers', or members of the royal affinity; and 'guests', those members of the aristocracy who participated in the cultural and political activities centred on the person of the king. By distinguishing between these three groups and assessing their relative importance at different stages during the fourteenth and fifteenth centuries we may build up an impression of the nature and role of the court in the politics of the period.

Many of the staff of the royal household were minor functionaries employed in the major logistical challenge of providing comfortable quarters, good food and adequate transport for the king and his entourage. Such men (and almost all domestic servants *were* men) played only a passive role in politics by helping to swell the costs of the royal establishment and thus raising public consciousness of the extravagance of the court. The senior positions in the household, however, carried considerable political importance and were filled by men of knightly or even noble rank. The most interesting such office in our period is the post of chamberlain, which, because it carried special responsibility for the king's private apartments, gave its holder a great deal of discretion over who did, and who did not, have access to the person of the monarch. Under certain circumstances the chamberlain could became quite literally a physical barrier between the king and the members of the aristocracy in attendance at his court.[3]

The most controversial of the chamberlain's responsibilities, however, concerned the administration of patronage. Already under Edward II, the younger Despenser was accused of using his office as chamberlain to secure honours for his father.[4] During the dotage of Edward III and the nonage of Richard II this informal influence developed bureaucratic recognition when successive chamberlains assumed the power to endorse petitions and sign warrants authorising the chancellor to issue documents under the great seal.[5] Out of this developed a whole system for the management of royal patronage, in which the chamberlain, along with the king's secretary (the keeper of the signet), administered the growing tide of petitions formally reserved for the personal attention of the monarch. The notoriety that attached to the role of the chamberlain in the late fourteenth century (William Latimer was impeached in the Good Parliament, while two of Richard II's chamberlains, Simon Burley and William Scrope, were put to death) made the early Lancastrian regime rather more circumspect both in the selection of personnel and in the use of the signet, sign manual and chamberlains' endorsements as direct authority for grants of patronage.[6] The return during Henry VI's majority rule to a more arbitrary system of authorisations was therefore almost bound to raise suspicion. By the 1440s, moreover, members of the household such as John Trevelyan and Walter Daniel were quite openly selling their services as brokers to those suitors requiring access to the king's grace. Although chamber *politics* is a phenomenon more usually associated with the Yorkists and Tudors, chamber *patronage* therefore became a significant, and at times emotive, issue in political life from at least the time of Richard II.

The second element within the court, the king's retainers, are conveniently distinguished from the household proper by the fact that, although they were contracted to serve the monarch, they did not reside permanently with him but operated from their own bases in the provinces. Their claim to be regarded as courtiers might therefore seem rather tenuous were it not for the fact that the 'court' was seen as a cultural and political phenomenon as well as a domestic institution with a defined physical location.[7] In a formal sense, at least, the royal affinity did not emerge until the end of the fourteenth century. It was Richard II who first realised that the relationship between the crown and the gentry did not necessarily have to be mediated through the magnates and that the crown had the capacity to create a wider political constituency on which it might draw when its relationship with the nobility was less than perfect. Taking up the model of the great baronial retinues, Richard began to contract members of provincial landed society to his service; by the end of his reign, the royal affinity numbered over 150 knights and esquires, making it both larger and more widely distributed than any comparable aristocratic following.[8] Under different circumstances, this experiment might have been discredited by the manifest failure of the Ricardian retinue to protect the king from deposition in 1399. But the accession of Henry IV had the effect of bringing the greatest noble affinity, that of John of Gaunt, into the direct service of the crown. The result was that the king now had not only by far the largest political following in the country, amounting to 250–300 knights and esquires, but also, again, the one with the greatest geographical range. By the accidents of inheritance, Henry IV and Henry V were therefore committed to the maintenance of a new royal following in the provinces.

The cost-effectiveness of this policy is not altogether easy to judge. There was nothing exclusive about the royal affinity, and many of its members associated freely with other baronial retinues.[9] On the other hand, there are obvious reasons for assuming that service to the king normally took precedence: not only did the crown offer larger annuities than most noblemen, it also had an infinitely larger store of political patronage through its control over the major offices of local government. This, together with the obvious prestige derived from wearing the king's livery badges (the white hart under Richard II and the collar of SS under the Lancastrians) and from the family and friendship networks that linked many members of the royal affinity with their counterparts in the household, served to establish an effective 'court' presence in places far removed from the king's normal places of residence. By extension, the threat posed to the royal affinity by the unexpected death of Henry V was also one of the major challenges to the stability of the Lancastrian regime. Since the good lordship and generous disposition of patronage that were so essential to the maintenance of any affinity were precisely the features of kingship that could not be exercised by substitutes during a minority, the management of the retinue became one of the greatest political problems of the 1420s and 1430s.

Consequently, by the time that Henry VI (or those about him) began to dispense the royal grace again in the 1440s, the Lancastrian affinity seems largely to have disintegrated and the sort of patronage that had created and upheld a royal following in the provinces under Richard II, Henry IV and Henry V was now being directed increasingly towards those who were already formally employed as members of the royal household. In one sense, then, the distinction between the household and the affinity, the 'employees' and the 'retainers', simply broke down towards the end of our period. But far from resolving tensions, this process had the effect of disturbing the delicate balance previously maintained between the central and local manifestations of the court.[10] The 1440s witnessed a very remarkable increase in the number of household men holding office as sheriffs and justices of the peace. This intrusion into an appointments system that was normally so sensitive to local political elites was inevitably seen as far more of a threat than the 'natural' processes by which members of the royal affinity functioning in the provinces had earlier succeeded to office. Far from uniting the central and local elements of the court, then, Henry VI's reliance on employees rather than retainers simply exacerbated the already considerable controversy surrounding his patronage and the unpopularity of his court.

The third and final group that made up the membership of the royal court during the fourteenth and fifteenth centuries – the 'guests' – were in many ways the most important, though ironically the nature of the evidence now makes them the most difficult to identify. Although a small number of the peerage held office in the household, it was extremely rare for noblemen to reside with the king. On the other hand, the tendency during the late fourteenth and fifteenth centuries for the royal household (and, to a lesser extent, the king himself) to settle for long periods in the royal palaces in and around the capital – Westminster, Kennington, Windsor, Sheen, Eltham, and so on – inevitably encouraged the high aristocracy (and, indeed, many members of the gentry) to gravitate towards the court. That a growing number of noblemen began to keep permanent town houses during this period is indeed an important sign of the emergence of London and Westminster as a political and cultural as well as a purely administrative, financial and judicial capital.[11]

The witness lists appended to royal charters provide the best available guide to the names of those magnates who were regarded as intimates of the king and frequenters of the court. This evidence indicates that whereas the courts of Edward III (until the 1370s) and Henry V (after 1414) drew from a fairly wide aristocratic base, that of Richard II was dominated, particularly after the mid-1390s, by a narrow clique of king's friends, including some of the main beneficiaries of the sudden outpouring of Ricardian patronage in 1397: John Beaufort, marquis of Somerset, John Montague, earl of Salisbury, Aubrey de Vere, earl of Oxford, and Thomas Despenser, earl of Gloucester.[12] The accidental or deliberate ostracising of the rest of the established nobility inevitably bred a sense of alienation that could, in the extreme circumstances of Henry VI's majority rule, erupt into full-scale political conflict. In fact, the administrative sources indicate that Henry's court remained relatively open for most of the 1440s: it was only the defeats in France in 1449–50 that created a major crisis of confidence and forced the nobility to distance itself from the discredited regime.[13] It was this withdrawal, however, that also allowed those outside the immediate royal circle to lay the blame for the controversies and failures of recent years on Suffolk, and, in particular, to represent the duke of York's earlier appointment to the lieutenancy of Ireland in 1447 as a means of exiling him from the king's circle and the seat of power.[14] Clearly, the court was not only a powerful political institution but an increasingly important political *issue* in late medieval England.

The Council

The aristocratic presence in the court provided the vital link between the household and the council, between the internal wranglings over patronage that were the stuff of chamber politics and the great matters of state that preoccupied the king's chief ministers. It is anachronistic to speak of the council as a monolithic institution in this period: the term was as likely to be applied to the act of giving advice (the modern sense of 'counselling') as to any organised and defined group of 'councillors'. In many respects, indeed, the idealised image of the council in the late Middle Ages remained rooted in the tradition of governance through informal consensus. Like the court, then, the council can only be understood by appreciating its various constituent parts.

The different manifestations of the council are perhaps best appreciated by a comparison between the two most extreme applications of the term. The real heart of the council lay in a small committee of chief ministers, led by the chancellor, the treasurer and (at least from the later fourteenth century) the keeper of the privy seal, meeting regularly at Westminster during the legal and financial terms to take executive decisions and organise the implementation of policy through the relevant departments. At the other end of the scale were great councils, special meetings of some or all of the parliamentary peerage, to which the crown might also summon knights, burgesses, merchants or any other group that had an immediate interest in the extraordinary business in hand. Between these two extremes was an almost infinite number of variations on the conciliar theme, the balance between them depending to a large extent on the king's own circumstances: whether he was of age, whether he was at home or abroad, whether he preferred to command or to consult, and so on. The political implications of these constant shifts of emphasis were profound, and the politics of the later Middle Ages has often been characterised in terms of a struggle between the crown, seeking to preserve its freedom to nominate ministers and select counsellors, and the nobility, striving to gain guaranteed representation in the processes of governmental decision-making. In fact, an important distinction needs to be drawn between the sorts of baronial councils envisaged at moments of political crisis and the more gradual and subtle shifts that came about in the balance between the ministerial and the aristocratic elements within the inner circles of the king's council. This is best demonstrated by a brief chronological survey of the evolution of the king's council from 1300 to 1450.

The idea of an aristocratic body acting as a watchdog upon the king and his ministers and enjoying some degree of coercive power over both had become a fairly regular part of the package of constitutional concessions demanded at moments of high political tension under John and Henry III. It does not follow, however, that the nobility sought to be permanently involved in the day-to-day business of governing the realm: medieval magnates had better things to do with their time than to deal with mere bureaucracy. This is demonstrated very clearly in the mechanisms by which the Ordainers of 1310–11 proposed to guarantee the implementation of their reforms. Ignoring or rejecting the elaborate schemes for a standing baronial council devised in 1258, the Ordainers placed their trust in parliament. All the great business of the realm – the making of war, the distribution of major patronage, the appointment of the chief officers of state – was to be undertaken by the king 'with the common assent of his baronage, and that in parliament'.[15] Otherwise, there was to be no permanent structure by which the exercise of the royal prerogative might be checked or constrained. Ironically, and in contrast to the three parliaments a year demanded in the Provisions of Oxford of 1258, the Ordainers considered that one, or if necessary two, parliaments a year would be sufficient.[16] In the light of Edward II's obvious hostility to the Ordinances, it is easy to criticise such proposals as inadequate and naive, but it may be fairer to stress that the whole idea of a standing baronial commission had lost much of its credibility since the 1260s and that the leap of imagination required to turn the peerage into a kind of corporate agency of central government was simply too great for anyone to contemplate at this stage.

It may be, therefore, that the gradual integration of the magnates into the regular work of the king's council is best explained not in terms of a collective response to major constitutional emergencies but through the individual experiences of those noblemen who were drawn more closely into the deliberation of government policy in the administrative council. In some ways, the French wars of Edward III could be said to have encouraged this trend. During the king's absences on the continent, the kingdom was placed under the titular custody of one of his infant sons and the actual responsibilities of state were entrusted to a committee of prelates, ministers, earls and barons. The notable petition of the parliamentary commons in 1340 for 'certain peers', 'elected' in parliament, to 'supervise the business of the king and of the realm' and to be accountable to future parliaments for their actions should probably be interpreted in reference to such a regency council.[17] However, it is also worth pointing out that under Edward III, as later under Henry V, the very high rate of aristocratic participation in war limited the choice of regency councillors and actually provided the nobility with a distraction or welcome relief from the often rather mundane business of the council chamber.

In fact, the event that probably did most to encourage a greater baronial commitment to the regular business of state was the minority of Richard II. The appointment of a single individual as *rector* both of the king and of the kingdom had been rejected on the unexpected accession of the youthful Edward III in favour of a council of magnates and prelates acting as advisors to the ministers of state, but the effective take-over of government by Mortimer and Isabella had prevented this body from developing an authority of its own.[18] The councils appointed during the first three years of Richard II's reign were therefore the first properly to embody the idea of regency by commission. These committees, established in parliament, had four notable characteristics: they were intended to represent a fairly wide cross-section of the political elite by including bishops, earls, barons, knights banneret and knights bachelor; they were the first councils to be described as 'continual', denoting comprehensive responsibility for the administration of the realm; they were empowered to make policy decisions and to implement them through the departments of state; and their members were the first to be guaranteed expenses for the onerous duties they undertook in the king's service.[19] Ironically, it may have been the last of these novelties that encouraged the rather premature abandonment of continual councils in the cost-conscious parliament of January 1380. It is possible that the concept of a more institutionalised form of council outlived this stroke of policy and provided both impetus and justification for the various reform commissions foisted upon the young king during the 1380s, particularly that appointed in the Wonderful Parliament of 1386. But it is also very significant that, when he finally declared himself of age in May 1389, Richard II immediately asserted the monarch's traditional freedom to select his advisors at will.[20] The notion of a more formal council in which the aristocracy played an acknowledged role had, for the moment, been confounded.

It was this same notion, however, that led the parliamentary commons on at least four occasions under Henry IV – in 1401, 1404, 1406 and 1410 – to revive the demands of 1340 and petition that the council be appointed in parliament and made answerable there for its actions.[21] These requests gained impetus from a somewhat ironic belief that the best and wisest advice was to be had not from the members of the knightly class (including some former MPs), whom Henry had increasingly recruited for political service, but from a properly integrated and 'representative' body of ministers, bishops, nobles and knights akin to the minority councils of Richard II. It is also worth noting that the commons were deeply concerned over Henry's unpredictable and incapacitating bouts of 'leprosy' (now variously interpreted as syphilis, epilepsy or coronary heart disease) and may have been seeking to create a kind of regency council in waiting.[22] Because of his financial embarrassment, Henry IV had little room for manoeuvre, and for a year after the 1406 parliament the government of the realm was to all intents and purposes transferred from the king to his council. But this was just as much an infringement of the royal prerogative as the commission of 1386 had been, and after 1407 Henry IV would brook no further continual councils. Instead, a new aristocratic grouping, led by the prince of Wales and his Beaufort relatives, began to play an increasingly prominent part in the work of government. Although this, and the more informal system whereby Henry V subsequently secured the consent of the magnates for his foreign and domestic policies, represented something of a return to older traditions of baronial counsel, it is also apparent that the councils of the 1380s and 1400s had created something of a new culture of service among the political elite.[23] The increasing scope of the state was bringing aristocratic and bureaucratic government closer together, and the forum in which this alliance first manifested itself was the supreme advisory agency, the council.

These relatively new notions of regular aristocratic participation in the affairs of the centre naturally coalesced during the long minority administration of Henry VI. For an unprecedented period of fifteen years the government of England was conducted by a permanent commission of bishops, nobles, barons and knights nominated by the lords in parliament. It must be stressed that most of the more humdrum business was still done by the ministers in conjunction with a small and significant body of 'professional' councillors who had seen long service in the royal household.[24] Even so, the corporate commitment to this commission demonstrated not only by its own members but also by the wider parliamentary peerage in their regular resistance to the duke of Gloucester's bids to extend his limited role as protector into that of *rector* of the kingdom must at least in part have arisen from a growing confidence in its real ability to manage the realm. This is not to say that the council entertained the idea of permanently accroaching the king's power: the assumption was always that it would disband as soon as the boy-king asserted his right to rule. Ironically, what really perpetuated the notion of a conciliar commission was the fact that, unlike Edward III in 1330 or Richard II in 1389, Henry VI seemed incapable of such action.

The shift from conciliar to royal government was in fact a long and difficult process that began around 1432 in Gloucester's attempts to use the king as a means of subverting the council, and came to completion only around 1445 in the ascendancy of Suffolk.[25] The most important feature of this process lay in the fact that the transfer of authority seems to have been engineered not by the young Henry but by his courtiers. Under such circumstances, it is easy to see why the members of the original minority administration should have deemed it wise to secure the appointment of a new continual council at the very moment when the king was declared of age in 1437 and to have it endowed with executive as well as the more traditional advisory powers. The most striking result of this was that, although Henry VI was now empowered to dispense his grace at will, those members of the aristocracy seeking resolution of their disputes during the early 1440s looked to the council, rather than the throne, for assistance. Behind such shifts of attitude presumably lay the widespread belief that Henry was not actually responsible for his own actions and that the only defence against the gradual take-over of the whole government by the court lay in a regular and formal council properly representative of the political elite. It was this new and enduring belief that later underpinned the arrangements worked out in 1453–4 when Henry VI's collapse into a deep depression (a condition now usually identified as catatonic schizophrenia) necessitated the revival of a minority-style administration, with the duke of York taking the title of protector and a broadly based aristocratic council enjoying general responsibility for the king's government.[26] Thus, but for the king's unexpected recovery, would the kingdom presumably have been administered for the rest of Henry's life.

The period 1300–1450 may therefore be said to have witnessed a highly significant change in the relationship between the political elite and the king's council. For most of the fourteenth century the members of the nobility continued to interpret their obligation and privilege to act as the king's counsellors in a profoundly traditional way: barely recognising a distinction between the court and the council, they saw themselves not as servants of the state but as participants in its great matters. Contrastingly, by the fifteenth century the magnates were coming to appreciate that their political influence depended not merely on their historic function as leaders in the localities nor simply on personal association with the king in the social setting of the court but on their willingness to become directly involved in an increasingly formal and business-like council. The final stage in this process was reached when members of the high nobility themselves assumed the responsibilities of major office. It is not surprising that when, from the later fourteenth century, the crown began occasionally to appoint laymen to the two most important posts in central government, the chancellorship and treasurership, it tended at first to chose those whose families had themselves risen through government service: Sir Richard Scrope, treasurer from 1371 to 1375, is an early case in point. Similarly, in the first half of the fifteenth century, the majority of lay ministers of state still tended to come from the ranks of the lesser baronial and knightly families closely linked to the Lancastrian household – men such as John Tiptoft, Henry Fitz-Hugh, Walter Hungerford and Ralph Cromwell, the last of whom was one of the longest-serving treasurers of the later Middle Ages (1433–43). Nevertheless, the appointment of Thomas Fitzalan, earl of Arundel, as Henry V's first treasurer and the installation of Richard Neville, earl of Salisbury, as chancellor during the emergency brought on by Henry VI's madness in 1454 were powerful political signals. The high nobility saw their position as counsellors no longer merely as a general privilege in accordance with their social status but as a very necessary function that provided the essential guarantee of their continued involvement in the political life of the realm.

Parliament

As with the court and council, so with parliament, the political institutions of the later Middle Ages emerged not according to some pre-ordained plan but through the pressures and accidents of circumstance. The origins of parliament are obscure and therefore remain controversial; nor is there complete unanimity about the functions, authority and influence of parliament in the late medieval state. It can in fact be argued that the reverential attitude adopted towards parliament since the constitutional struggles of the seventeenth century has tended to exaggerate the importance of this institution by isolating it from the much broader tradition of consultation and participation that characterised the lower levels of medieval public administration.[27] When the crown occasionally summoned to 'national' assemblies not only its traditional advisors among the lay and ecclesiastical tenants in chief but also (from 1212) knights and (from 1265) townsmen, it was not taking some revolutionary step towards modern principles of democracy but simply building on an existing base of government by representation. This interpretation has special importance in the present context, for it helps to explain how, during the later Middle Ages, parliament came to serve not simply as an agency of the state but as a crucial point of political contact between the crown and its subjects.

At the beginning of the fourteenth century the English parliament had not yet assumed all the attributes and functions that were to characterise its later history. The anonymous author of the *Modus tenendi parliamentum* ('The method of holding parliament'), writing in the early 1320s, saw parliament not in terms of lords and commons but as a series of estates listed according to conventional notions of the social hierarchy: lords spiritual, clerical proctors (representatives of the lower clergy), lords temporal, barons of the Cinque Ports, knights, citizens and burgesses.[28] He might also have included a further estate of ministers, the large number of senior officials, judges, clerks and household servants who participated in sessions of the king's parliament.[29] By the fifteenth century, in contrast, parliament had reached its developed form. The lower clergy had largely disappeared, and now met separately with the prelates in the two convocations of Canterbury and York. Parliament itself was perceived as incorporating only three estates, the lords spiritual, lords temporal and commons, organised into two houses of peers and representatives. Parliamentary procedure and terminology had also become surprisingly sophisticated: the appointment of speakers, the development of impeachment, the procedure for reading bills, the observation of majority rule and the beginnings of a notion of parliamentary privilege, all of which can be discerned in the fourteenth and fifteenth centuries, inevitably tend to create a strong impression of modernity. In fact, of course, the English parliament of the later Middle Ages differed in a fundamental way from its modern successor by having only a very tenuous link with government: parliament had no executive authority of its own and its decisions could only be implemented by the crown, acting through the secretarial, financial and judicial agencies of state. The fact that parliaments were called more frequently in the fourteenth and early fifteenth centuries than under the Yorkists and Tudors was a reflection not of any notable differences in the constitutional structure but of the simple fact that the Plantagenets and Lancastrians spent much longer periods at war and needed parliamentary subsidies to support their military enterprises.

It is natural, given the rise of the representative element during the fourteenth and fifteenth centuries, to focus the following discussion on the role of the commons in parliament. However, it is important to acknowledge, even if only in passing, that parliament was also a political forum for the high nobility. The fact that not all the lords temporal and spiritual actually turned up when summoned to parliament does not necessarily mean that the aristocracy as a whole was indifferent to, or marginalised from, the political debate within these assemblies.[30] It is particularly interesting to notice that both the crown and the commons continued to recognise that the provision of advice in parliament was the special responsibility of the lords: in the characteristic legal terminology of the Middle Ages, the commons were 'petitioners' or suitors, whereas the peers acted as advisors and judges, or 'counsel', to the king.[31] One important consequence of this was that the upper house continued to dominate parliamentary discussions over the making of war and peace: it was only when the crown sought parliamentary ratification for a formal policy to which it and the nobility were already committed, as at the opening of hostilities against France in 1337 and 1414 or on the formal confirmation of the treaties of Brétigny and Troyes, that the crown took particular concern to ensure that the whole of parliament, lords and commons alike, was associated (one might almost say implicated) in such great matters.[32]

Why, then, were the commons regarded, at least from the time of Edward III, as an essential part of parliament? The answer lies in the development from the late thirteenth century of two of the most important and exclusive functions of parliament: taxation and petitioning. It is well known that from the 1290s the crown sought to obtain formal consent to direct taxes not only from great councils of magnates but also from representatives of county and urban communities, thereby creating the kind of 'full' parliaments that were to be the norm from 1327 onwards. The reasons for this development are obvious enough: if taxation was to be universal, it was important in practical as well as philosophical terms to gain the consent, by proxy, of all the king's subjects (or at least, in less ambitious but more relevant terms, of those men belonging to the broadly-based political society identified in chapter 1).[33] But the development also had much wider constitutional implications. In 1297, and again in 1311, it was still the barons who regarded themselves as forming, or representing, the 'community of the realm' in political discussion or confrontation with the king.[34] By contrast, the author of the *Modus tenendi parliamentum*, when discussing taxation, argued that the lords in parliament could speak only for themselves and that it was the knights, citizens and burgesses who represented 'the whole community of England'.[35] This was both a partisan and, for its time, a very radical stance. Yet it is noticeable that after 1340 the lords in parliament never attempted to make unilateral grants of taxation binding on others outside the elite;[36] and by the end of the fourteenth century the official records of parliamentary subsidies no longer stated that taxes were granted by the lords and commons, but 'by the commons with the assent of the lords'.[37] In a fiscal context at least, there is no doubt that the commons had taken the lead in parliament and reduced the lords to a subordinate role. It is in the same context that we should probably also interpret the new, inclusive, application of the phrase 'community of the realm' that emerged in the course of the fourteenth century.

The second of the special powers accorded to parliament from the time of Edward I was the right to petition the crown.[38] In reality, of course, suitors could approach the king at any time: the images of Edward III receiving petitions while out hunting and Henry V dealing with complaints while taking his leisure after dinner are reminiscent of an older tradition stretching back to King Alfred, who gave judgments, it was said, while washing his hands.[39] However, Edward I's deliberate policy of encouraging his subjects to use sessions of parliament particularly as a means of complaining against the malpractices of his own ministers and local agents, together with his formal guarantee that all petitions received in parliament would be granted a response before the session ended, greatly increased both the number and the range of petitions received by the crown in parliament: over 500, for instance, in 1305. From an early stage, then, bureaucratic mechanisms had to be created to deal with such a mass of business and prevent king and council from becoming totally preoccupied with private concerns. Before long, private suitors realised that there were other extra-parliamentary channels that might more profitably be pursued, and the numbers of personal or 'singular' petitions presented in parliament were already declining markedly by the 1330s when, in a period of considerable diplomatic and military activity, parliamentary sessions were dominated by great matters of common concern to the kingdom.

At precisely the same time, however, a new prominence was also given to certain private petitions identified by their authors or by the clerks of parliament as being of general concern to particular areas, social groups or, indeed, to the realm as a whole. Before the reign of Edward II, there is no direct evidence that the commons, acting in concert, attempted to frame and forward similar requests for consideration as 'common' petitions. Indeed, when individual members of the commons sought to bring political issues to the attention of the government, they did so only as agents of the lords: this is what happened in the Lincoln Parliament of 1301 when Henry Keighley, knight of the shire for Lancashire, acted as spokesman for the barons (and, incidentally, suffered the consequences, being imprisoned by the king for his temerity).[40] From the 1310s, however, and particularly after 1322, when the aristocratic opposition to Edward II was effectively eliminated, the commons appear to have taken up the earlier practices of the nobility and clergy and begun to compile lists of grievances (*gravamina*) which were then presented directly to the crown in parliament. It was these petitions which, during Edward III's reign, came to be considered as 'common'; the definition of what was, and what was not, a matter of general concern now rested, in other words, not with the clerks of parliament but with the knights and burgesses themselves. From the 1340s, at the latest, the common petitions and the replies supplied by the king and council were regularly written up on the official record of parliamentary proceedings. Petitioning had therefore changed from an individual to a corporate act and common petitions had in effect become the petitions of the commons.[41] The particular status and authority enjoyed by the common petitions is demonstrated by the fact that the clergy of Canterbury province, who often met in convocation while parliament was sitting, made serious efforts in the first half of the fourteenth century to have their own *gravamina* included on the parliament roll: it is indeed one of the ironies of the clergy's withdrawal from parliament – which they regarded as a victory for ecclesiastical liberties – that the church became marginalised from the main political forum and found it increasingly difficult during the later fourteenth and fifteenth centuries to secure the kind of parliamentary co-operation that it now realised was so essential for the maintenance of its own interests.[42]

The final stage in the development of the parliamentary petition came when the commons, acting in a collective capacity, began to act as brokers for private individuals and corporations wishing to forward their interests in parliament. One of the earliest such cases is also one of the best known: when Thomas Haxey drew up his famous, and highly controversial, petition against the extravagances of Richard II's household in 1397 he put it up for adoption by the commons – though his hopes of securing immunity through anonymity were dashed and he, like Keighley before him, quickly became the focus of the king's wrath.[43] That sponsorship by the commons came to be regarded as the most effective way to secure the royal grace on less contentious matters is signified by the way the system was exploited in the fifteenth century not only by powerful interest groups such as the Company of the Staple at Calais but even by men at the very top levels of the political elite such as John, duke of Bedford, and Cardinal Beaufort. It was by such means that Richard, duke of York, also manipulated the commons into petitioning for recognition of his title as heir to the throne in 1451 – though once again the agent responsible for introducing the measure, York's counsellor Thomas Young, MP for Bristol, was imprisoned at the king's pleasure. Petitions, or 'bills' as they increasingly came to be known in the fifteenth century (the change in terminology is, in itself, of little significance), therefore provide an important example of the way in which parliament could be used both for public and private business, and indicate why the institution in general, and the commons in particular, were regarded as such an essential part of the political structure.

The impact of such developments is best appreciated by the link established between taxation and petitioning; in other words, the way in which the commons were able to use their exclusive control over taxation as a way of putting pressure on the crown to redress their grievances. Under Edward I, when the magnates took responsibility for articulating the complaints of the community, parliaments proved remarkably confident about setting political conditions on grants of supply: witness the way in which the king's requests for money to support the Scottish war were held up for some eighteen months in 1300-1 as a result of his reluctance to accept the conditions represented by the Articles upon the Charters and the *gravamina* forwarded by Henry Keighley. When the commons first took over both as the arbiters of taxation and as the mouthpiece of the political community, they proved notably more reticent about making such connections, at least explicitly: although, like the clergy, they frequently set conditions on the way in which a tax was to be collected, it was only in moments of extreme political conflict and in the knowledge that the lords would support their stand – as in 1340 – that the knights and burgesses felt able to demand remedies for their political grievances as an actual condition of the grant of supply.[44] During the later fourteenth century, however, it became the practice for the commons to deliver their petitions first and delay the confirmation of the tax until the final day of the assembly, when the crown's responses to bills were read out in plenary session. Although the commons' request in 1401 for a statement of the king's answers *before* the delivery of the tax was rebuffed, it is evident that a considerable amount of back-stage bargaining was now going on before the formalities of the final day. This, indeed, is one of the main reasons why meetings of parliament became so much more protracted during the later fourteenth and fifteenth centuries: the Good Parliament of 1376 (10 weeks), the aptly named Long Parliament of 1406 (a total of 23 weeks over three sessions) and the un-named, but equally remarkable, parliament of 1445-6 (27 weeks in four sessions) all outlived their natural span largely because of the repeated refusal of the commons to concede adequate offers of taxation.[45]

The most striking demonstration of parliament's ability to use its financial powers as a means of securing political concessions lay in the control it came to enjoy over the making of statutory legislation. Just as the term 'parliament' only gradually hardened into specific usage during the late thirteenth and early fourteenth centuries, so also did the word 'statute' have a much broader application at the start than at the end of this period.[46] It was only during the first half of the fourteenth century that statutes, those particularly solemn, far-reaching and eternal statements of law published (that is, sent out for proclamation) by the king and council, came to be regarded as valid only if first promulgated in a properly constituted parliament. More significantly, it was in precisely the same period that the statutes came more and more to incorporate the crown's responses to common petitions, thus providing a tangible expression of the ability of the knights and burgesses to initiate changes in the administrative, judicial and economic organisation of the realm. For most of the fourteenth century, the commons' role was to highlight grievances, not to dictate answers: it was up to the king, in association with the legal experts of his council, to frame remedial legislation in response to their general requests. By 1450, however, two important changes had come about. First, legislation proposed either by the crown or by the lords was put into the form of a bill and always referred to the commons for approval before going on to be made up into a statute; and secondly, the resulting common petitions showed an increasing tendency to specify the precise remedy that ought to appear in the resulting statute. The degree of parliamentary initiative thus implied is still something of an open question, since the available documentation does not always allow us to discern between official, lords' and commons' bills and therefore to calculate their relative take-up as statutes.[47] Nevertheless, there are obviously strong grounds for arguing that the legislative influence of parliament, and more particularly of the commons, was indeed transformed over the century and a half from Edward I to Henry VI.

This chapter has sought to demonstrate how the central political institutions of the late medieval state developed in response to the challenges of government and altered significantly both in their composition and in their influence. The court impinged in a new way on the regions through the creation of a royal affinity in the shires, while the crown's need for war finance transformed parliament from a predominantly aristocratic body into a representative assembly drawing its membership from the provincial landed gentry and the merchant classes. Even the council, which remained the most exclusive political assembly in the land, experienced important changes as the nobility sought to maintain political pre-eminence by involving itself more systematically in the making of high policy. Furthermore, the increasing self-confidence of parliament – and particularly of the parliamentary commons – meant that the composition and influence of both the court and the council became in themselves major topics of political debate. The extent to which that debate impinged on the consciousness of the lower reaches of provincial political society is a subject that will be picked up at the end of the next chapter. For the present, we may conclude that during the period 1300–1450 the central institutions not only responded directly to the course of political events but also drew into their membership and general sphere of influence a larger cross-section of political society than had ever previously engaged in high politics. Above all, parliament became the natural environment in which the community of the realm entered into direct political dialogue with the crown on the issues that were of greatest concern to the country as a whole. That parliament was to be of considerably less importance and relevance to the political life of the later fifteenth and sixteenth centuries serves only to reinforce the point that the period covered by this book has its own discrete political character.

3

POLITICAL IDENTITIES: THE LOCALITIES

In recent years there has been a reaction against the history of 'high' politics (that is, as viewed from the centre) and towards the idea that the true character of medieval political life can only be comprehended by studying the 'low' politics of the regions and localities and the 'popular' politics of the mob. This approach has undoubtedly transformed our understanding of the complexity and richness of medieval political culture. Unfortunately, however, it has all too often been seen as replacing, rather than supplementing, the study of central politics and has sometimes given the impression that later medieval England was rather like France: a patchwork of local polities that saw the king's actions as at best an irrelevance, at worst an intrusion, into the affairs of the provincial power elites. This is to forget not only the intensity and uniformity of English royal government in the Middle Ages but also the development of centralised political institutions with the capacity to represent the interests of the provinces at the very heart of political life. In examining local institutions and attitudes, we shall therefore need to understand not only their internal mechanisms and particular preoccupations but also the degree to which these were linked into a wider political system at the regional and national levels.

Since the principal purpose of this chapter is to establish the nature and degree of local political influence enjoyed by different groups of the king's subjects, it is organised according to the orders of society rather than by the formal institutions in which they operated. This approach has the advantage of demonstrating how those institutions – the courts of the shire, borough, hundred, vill and manor – could themselves be influenced by a variety of different social and political interests. But it is also intended to imply that a good deal of the political life of the localities took place not, in fact, in these public arenas but in much more informal, private or domestic contexts: indeed, it seems more than likely that the bonds of family, friendship, neighbourhood, religion and lordship could have just as formative an influence on political attitudes as any degree of participation in public administration.

The Peasantry

In one sense, the political perceptions of the mass of the English peasantry were still dominated in the later Middle Ages not by the state but by seigneurial authority: it was in the private court of the manor that the bulk of peasant litigation was undertaken, the majority of the peasants' petty offences punished and, most significantly, the interests and authority of the lord upheld. It was not until the sixteenth century that the crown intruded decisively into this level of government and in the process shifted the political consciousness of the rural population decisively from the private to the public sphere. In another respect, however, the fourteenth and fifteenth centuries may be said to have marked the essential period of transition between these poles. Several aspects of the process will be discussed later, in chapters 5 and 6: the invasions (and subsequent retreat) of royal tax collectors and commissioners of array; the emergence of the justices of the peace as royal agents charged to maintain order in the shires; and the increasing use of the king's justice to resolve private disputes between, or involving, peasants. For present purposes, it is necessary to focus on the social, administrative and political structures existing at the local level that allowed the peasantry – and particularly the peasant elite – to articulate its response to such developments.

In the fourteenth and fifteenth centuries there were large numbers of peasants whose formal legal status (in the case of villeins) or low economic standing (in the case of poor husbandmen and labourers) normally prevented them from participating actively in the local agencies of royal government, the courts of the vill, hundred and shire.[1] This is not to say, of course, that such groups lacked political perception. Since the nobility and gentry were comparatively small in number, absentee lordship was common – even the norm – and a great many manor and village communities had become conditioned to organising their own affairs without the direct exercise of seigneurial authority. Indeed, when lordship did intervene it could be a disruptive and controversial force, provoking the peasantry into concerted opposition.[2] Not surprisingly, then, the feudal reaction launched by the proprietary classes in the aftermath of the Black Death encouraged peasant communities to develop existing mechanisms of resistance. The simplest option was to run away, and there is plenty of evidence from the later fourteenth and fifteenth centuries to show that both villein tenants and free labourers become more inclined to withdraw their services when they deemed the liabilities of lordship or their terms of employment to be unreasonable. More significant for present purposes is the appeal of ancient demesne, the particular process whereby unfree peasants living on land that had once been in the king's hands were permitted to petition the crown for protection or redress against the oppressions of their current lord. In 1376–8 (the very period when the post-plague seigneurial reaction was possibly most intense) no fewer than forty villages made such appeals to the governments of Edward III and Richard II; this concentration of activity gives some credence to the otherwise rather hysterical references to the conspiracies of villein tenants made in the parliament of 1377.[3] The idea that the Peasants' Revolt of 1381 was itself made possible by the existence of a 'great society' reminiscent of modern underground and mass movements has long been discredited, but at least some recent work has stressed how the rebels were able to use their knowledge of the workings of local government – at the level of the hundred as well as the vill – to mobilise support and muster their forces.[4] (The inquiries launched by the crown in 1388–9 into the activities of English guilds may also have arisen from an enduring suspicion that religious and economic associations could provide a cloak for collective subversive activity.[5]) Finally, it should be pointed out that from Edward I's time the crown increasingly drew villein tenants into its orbit, making them liable for military service and royal taxation and, under certain conditions at least, employing them as jurors to supply the administrative information, as well as the judicial indictments, on which so much of the basic structure of the medieval state rested. When, in the fifteenth century, the common law courts began to recognise litigation concerning copy-hold tenancies (the successors to the customary tenancies held by villeins in the high Middle Ages) the state took yet another step towards the transcendent authority it was to claim over the rural population in later ages.[6]

The impact of such developments on the political attitudes of the peasantry will be discussed at the end of this chapter. Rather more has to be said at this stage about the particular political role of the yeomanry. The growth of royal government in the twelfth and thirteenth centuries had placed a remarkable range of re-sponsibilities in the hands of the most substantial members of village communities. They were regularly called upon to act as jurors and chief pledges, to organise local peace-keeping and tax collection, to take office as constables and bailiffs of vills and hundreds and to attend the courts of these ancient administrative units. In their capacity as freeholders and village representatives they also received summonses to the sessions of the shire court. It seems reasonable to assume that these men were in practice responsible for articulating the political ideas expressed in the large numbers of petitions from individual villages addressed to the crown from Edward I's reign onwards.[7] One striking example of this form of communication is found in a series of petitions dating from the later 1340s which complain about the malicious activities of tax collectors and the distress encountered as a result of the death or absence of some of the former principal taxpayers in particular rural communities.[8] Rather than pursuing such evi-dence in detail, however, it may be more instructive here to examine the possibility that the minor freeholders were not only the natural leaders of the peasantry but also direct participants in the political life of the upper orders.

The most obvious and important material on which to base such a discussion comes from the attendance records of the county courts. In the course of the fourteenth and fifteenth centuries the judicial functions of these assemblies declined as the shire court – meeting once every four or six weeks – began to develop more of the attributes of a political gathering.[9] Much of our evidence on attendance comes from what the modern historian at least would undoubtedly regard as the most 'political' of all activities, the election of parliamentary representatives. In 1406, in an attempt to guarantee that the sheriffs should not rig such elections, it was laid down by statute that the names of all those present in the county court at the time of the election be communicated to the central government. The numbers of electors preserved in the returns vary considerably, not only from county to county but also from election to election, and the variations have to be accounted for as much by erratic record-keeping as by differences in local attitudes to the importance of parliament. We have also to confront the awkward truth that the vast majority of returns named only men of quality and substance: the sort of people that we are attempting to trace here are all too often effectively lost in the phrase *et aliorum*, which often appears at the end of such lists.[10] Nevertheless, where they are apparently complete, and when they have been subjected to detailed analysis, these returns do indeed indicate that the largest group present at elections in the county courts was drawn from the ranks of the small freeholders.[11]

It does not follow, of course, that this numerical supremacy denoted political primacy. It would be blatantly foolish to argue that the landed elite did not enjoy the greatest influence in elections that were often arranged by informal private treaty between the sheriff and the comparatively small group of shire gentry from which the knights of the shire were normally selected (the property qualification imposed on county MPs by a parliamentary statute of 1445 simply confirmed what was already a reality and gave the gentry a formal monopoly over such posts). Indeed, it must be stressed that it was usually only in the rare event of a contested election that the yeomen came into play as active participants and the resulting lists of named attestors ran into hundreds rather than the more usual tens. The resulting concern of the upper orders over the possibility that the county court might be packed by rival candidates in contested elections probably provides the background to a statute of 1413 requiring that both electors and MPs should be resident in the relevant shires, as well as to the famous legislation of 1429–30 restricting the county franchise to freeholders with land to the value of at least 40s. a year. Considering that it was intended to preserve an oligarchy presumed to be under threat from the rabble, however, it is all the more remarkable that the latter measure set the property qualification so comparatively low, at a level that comfortably accommodated a large proportion of the yeomanry (a similar point can be made about the earlier statute of 1414 that fixed the 40s. freehold as a necessary qualification for jurors acting in cases of homicide and property disputes). It therefore appears that both the parliamentary commons, who campaigned for such legislation, and the crown, which promulgated it, were prepared to accept that minor freeholders had a rightful if still obviously subsidiary part to play in the political life of the shires.

Townsmen

The emergence of self-governing towns in the high Middle Ages had resulted in the growth of some extremely sophisticated systems of urban representation and administration. Furthermore, the independent status of cities and boroughs gave townsmen a particularly acute sense of their own constitutional identity. The recent proliferation of individual studies of medieval English towns, while making it increasingly difficult to generalise about either their economic fortunes or their governmental systems, has also helped to demonstrate the many different contexts in which political activity took place and political consciousness was nurtured. Participation in public affairs was measured not merely by admission to the freedom of the town (the urban equivalent of the franchise) and slow progression through the hierarchy of public office from the common council to the mayoralty, but also by membership of the numerous social and political networks represented among the craft guilds and religious fraternities that grew up particularly in the later fourteenth and fifteenth centuries. The most powerful manifestation of this multi-textured polity was the feast of Corpus Christi, in early summer, when the members of the political, economic and religious associations within many English towns processed through the streets in a symbolic affirmation of their natural superiority over the passive masses looking on from the sidelines.[12] Finally, the particular intensity and complexity of urban administration – which itself came to be seen in the economic depressions of the fifteenth century as a burdensome responsibility – made a high proportion of the urban population keenly aware of the character and course of politics within their own communities: the constitutional history of late medieval towns has frequently been characterised in terms of an on-going tension between 'oligarchical' and 'democratic' forms of government.[13]

What, then, of the possibility that the towns were also engaged in wider local, regional, or national political networks? It is clear that towns were primarily preoccupied with their own often tumultuous internal affairs: the urban uprisings of 1381 – whether at York, Scarborough and Beverley, or in St Albans, Cambridge and Bury St Edmunds – can all be explained largely in terms of local issues and local factions and appear to have had a good deal less concern with the more general political grievances that precipitated the simultaneous rural revolts.[14] However, despite their constitutional autonomy, towns clearly did not exist in political, any more than economic, isolation. A number of the more prestigious urban guilds of the later Middle Ages, such as St George's at Norwich, Corpus Christi at Boston, Holy Trinity at Coventry, and Holy Cross at Stratford upon Avon, drew their membership not simply from the civic elite but from gentry, nobility and even royalty with interests in the relevant regions. In particular, it is important to acknowledge that the towns only preserved their rights and interests through constant contact with the feudal lords who had originally granted their freedom, and above all with the greatest of those lords, the crown. The entries in surviving fourteenth- and fifteenth-century chamberlains' accounts (those of Norwich, Leicester, Exeter and York provide some good examples) recording fees and gifts to royal officials and to lawyers specifically retained to represent the relevant town in the central courts at Westminster provide striking evidence of the sort of channels through which provincial towns now maintained their political dialogue with the centre. And the series of petitions by which impoverished towns sought the partial or total remission of the annual fee farms payable to the royal exchequer during the reign of Henry VI speaks much for the common agenda, the concerted action, and the particularly successful lobbying that characterises the political relations between the towns and the crown in this period.[15]

The most important example of the integration of the towns into the wider political community of the later Middle Ages is, however, provided by their representation and participation in parliament. Since the crown only began to summon townsmen to national assemblies from the time of Henry III, and only regularly included citizens and burgesses in parliament after 1327, the attitude of the urban elites to their parliamentary responsibilities takes on particular importance for the period covered by this book. It used to be thought that the towns were indifferent to their right to separate representation since the records of central government imply imperfect attendance, and the social profiles of MPs suggest that borough seats were increasingly taken over by 'foreign' lawyers and gentry. It has been known for some time, however, that the attendance rates of the citizens and burgesses were actually very high and that towns were prepared to pay handsomely for such representation; it has also recently been argued that the 'invasion' of the boroughs in the fifteenth century, far from indicating the political passivity of the urban elites, signified their desire to be represented by men with the social status and political expertise necessary to defend the town's interests adequately in the king's parliaments.[16] It is significant that when, in 1372, concern was expressed about the way in which certain MPs tended to promote private rather than public interests in parliament, the crown banned lawyers only from representing the *shire* communities: there was clearly a widespread acceptance that urban representatives in parliament were entitled and expected to do business for their own constituents.[17] But if this goes a long way to explaining the value attached to parliamentary representation, it is also true that the citizens and burgesses in the commons were capable of concerted action. The townsmen may have continued to be treated as socially and politically inferior to the knights of the shire, and the political programme of the commons may well have been dominated by the preoccupations of the landed interest, but there are important indications, as we shall see in chapter 5, that the urban and mercantile communities were also capable of influencing both the agenda of parliament and, by extension, the policies of the state. Thus were townsmen integrated into the mainstream of political life in later medieval England.

The County Communities

We come now to what is regarded in much modern historical writing as the real heart of late medieval political society, the gentry. It is obviously tempting, and therefore dangerous, to assume that all those who claimed gentility regarded themselves as forming a particular social order with its own political identity and agenda: the elite corps of knights and wealthy esquires who dominated office-holding at the shire level and mixed freely with the provincial baronage must inevitably have had a very different outlook from the minor gentlemen whose natural milieu was the manor and the village.[18] In discussing the political networks of the gentry in the later Middle Ages, however, historians have concentrated rather less on these divisions and more on the structures that supposedly created a sense of unity – and perhaps of oligarchy – within the ranks of the greater or 'county' gentry. The result has been the creation of two rival camps: those who see gentry politics as having been organised along 'horizontal' lines and who identify the most powerful political institution in the so-called county community; and those who emphasise the primary influence of 'vertical' associations created between the nobility and the lesser landed classes, represented most typically by the baronial affinity. To resolve the resulting dichotomy it is necessary to recognise that there was a genuine plurality of experience in the provinces: the notion upon which this book is based, that England was in essence

47

a single polity, does not exclude the very obvious fact that political society was organised in different ways at the local level. In addition, however, it has to be stressed that lordship was much more pervasive a force than is often appreciated in studies of social organisation during the later Middle Ages. Although the following discussion of gentry politics separates the horizontal from the vertical associations as a matter of convenience, it is not intended to suggest either that they were exclusive or that one was notably more important than the other.

The existence of a county community in late medieval England may be said to have depended on two things. First, it was necessary to have a strong sense of administrative and cultural identity within the shire. The fact that English local government had operated at least from the tenth century within the context of the county meant that the holders of royal office were inevitably conditioned to the idea that this unit provided their natural sphere of activity and influence. This attitude became more deeply ingrained from the mid-thirteenth century when the increasing sophistication of royal government demanded that the king's principal local agents, the sheriffs, be assisted by a growing number of new local officials: escheators, assessors and collectors of taxes, and keepers and justices of the peace. On the other hand, it should be remembered that the government of the shires did not always operate in isolation: in a number of cases, for example, the sheriffdoms of two counties were combined (Essex and Hertfordshire, Oxfordshire and Berkshire, and so on) and the centres of influence within these twinned shires gravitated back and forth over their common boundaries according to the place of residence of the current sheriff. This also reminds us that the county boundary was rarely a barrier to those social and cultural networks, based on the ties of property, marriage and friendship, which did so much to create gentry communities in this and other periods. The county only seems to have provided a meaningful *cultural* identity where strong historical traditions and/or geographical isolation created a particular sense of otherness. This may have been the case in the 'ancient' shires of southern and eastern England, based as they were on Anglo-Saxon tribal associations; it was almost certainly the case in the linguistically distinct north-east, north-west, and south-west. The resulting mixture of cosmopolitan and provincial influences that characterises the gentry culture of this period is nicely demonstrated by some of the alliterative poems of the fourteenth century, such as *William of Palerne* and *Sir Gawain and the Green Knight*, in which sophisticated literary conventions culled from the French romance tradition were made accessible to a polite, but provincial, audience through the Middle English dialects and distinct literary traditions of the west and north-west midlands.[19]

The second feature that we would expect to find in a county community worthy of the name is an institution capable of representing gentle society and providing a forum in which the landed classes could articulate their political concerns. The county court is often assumed to have fulfilled this function in the later Middle Ages,[20] and we have already seen how, under certain circumstances – that is, in the context of contested parliamentary elections – this assembly could draw together a very significant proportion of the polity resident within the shire. High attendance was certainly not restricted to elections: in 1388, for instance, 330 of the 'better born and worthy' of Lincolnshire, along (interestingly) with 66 townsmen, came together, presumably in the county court, to declare their loyalty to the Lords Appellant.[21] It is not at all clear, however, that either the gentry or the minor freeholders turned out in large numbers to sessions for which no such exciting or extraordinary political business was tabled. The tidy-minded historian will inevitably try to rationalise the resulting variations. It may be possible, for instance, to distinguish between the low attendance rates in a shire such as Warwickshire or Leicestershire whose elites had interests that took them outside its boundaries (not least into other county courts) and the higher degree of participation demonstrated by the gentry in relatively self-contained, if not isolated, areas such as Norfolk and Suffolk.[22] Equally, it can be argued that the sheer size of the county (as in the case of Yorkshire) or the lack of a fixed headquarters for meetings of its court (as in Kent, Sussex, Cornwall and elsewhere) resulted in relatively low attendances.[23] Rather than explaining away their absences, however, it may be more satisfactory to suggest that most of the gentry were naturally disinclined to attend the county court unless they had private business to conduct there and that the regular attenders were drawn from a relatively small group particularly active in the administration and public affairs of the locality. It was this hard-core of local political figures that may also have been responsible for using the sessions of the county court as the opportunity to articulate and register local concerns in petitions formally addressed to the king and council in the name of the relevant shire communities. These petitions, which still survive in significant numbers in the Public Record Office, remind us once again that local assemblies existed not in isolation but as part of a hierarchy of representation and governance culminating in parliament and the crown.

The county court was not necessarily the only formal institution capable of bringing together the leading members of the gentry at a local level. It has been suggested that the sessions of the justices of assize and (from the later fourteenth century) the quarter sessions of the justices of the peace also provided a natural opportunity for the landed classes to express their solidarity.[24] The problem with such an argument, however, is that it appears to pre-empt the very important expansion in the administrative and economic responsibilities of the justices of the peace during the late fifteenth and sixteenth centuries and the concomitant increase in the size of the county bench, both of which helped to make the quarter sessions the real meeting place of the county community by the age of Elizabeth.[25] Close study of the peace sessions in East Anglia, Nottinghamshire and Yorkshire during the late fourteenth and the first half of the fifteenth centuries has revealed that only a small proportion of the shire elite formally included on the bench actually sat as justices and that most of the work was left to smaller groups of minor landholders and lawyers.[26] Once again, then, it seems that the gentry would only usually attend the peace session – and, by implication, the assizes – when they had their own business to pursue. In the continuing search for the collectivities that allowed the greater gentry to speak for their county communities, it may indeed be that we shall have to turn away from the shire courts and the quarter sessions and give far more attention to the informal gatherings – based around family celebrations and other feasts, tournaments and hunting parties, or property and other legal transactions – which were the real stuff of social intercourse for the landed classes of later medieval England.

The Baronial Affinity

The principal manifestations of the 'vertical' organisation of local gentry societies were the retinues or affinities maintained by the nobility. These retinues consisted of several recognisable, if over-lapping, groups: an inner core of estate managers, household officials and servants; an intermediate band formed by those – mainly gentry and lawyers – who were formally retained in the service of the lord but did not reside with him; and an outer circle of 'well wishers', who were not necessarily contracted to the lord but were prepared to accept – and exploit – his social and political primacy in the region.[27] It used to be thought that baronial affinities had their origins in the military contracts and sub-contracts used since the late thirteenth century for the recruitment of men at arms to royal armies. However, the fact that there was comparatively little overlap between the peace-time and the war-time retinues of the late medieval aristocracy helps to give greater credence to a new approach that sees indentures of retainer as part of a more general trend, also evident from the thirteenth century, towards the use of written agreements to create a wide range of political, tenurial, and occupational relationships.[28] While the Hundred Years War presumably had some role to play in rein-forcing the new patron–client relationship within the much older context of the war band, the late medieval retinue should not therefore be seen primarily as a military force: the idea that fifteenth-century noblemen were capable of mounting a civil war merely by mobilising their gentry retainers has certainly been rejected in modern studies of military organisation during the Wars of the Roses.[29] Indeed, although the growth of the aris-tocratic affinity can certainly be explained in terms of the nobility's awareness of the political value attached to lordship, it is becoming more and more apparent that the main beneficiaries of 'bastard feudalism' were not the patrons but the clients.

How widespread and powerful, then, was this phenomenon? It

has sometimes been implied by those who favour the horizontal approach to late medieval politics that the gentry in some way preferred to be independent of noble influence, strongly resisting baronial interference and stoutly defending the tradition of local autonomy.[30] The problem with this approach is that while self-regulating gentry societies were quite normal in the late Middle Ages, they were not necessarily considered normative. Since the hierarchy was divinely ordained, individuals found it natural to express their social and political status not only in terms of those placed below them but also in reference to their superiors. To be within the affinity of a great nobleman – or of the king – was therefore to be a person of rank and importance: as contemporaries would have put it, to enjoy both 'good lordship' and 'worship'.[31] The same prevailing attitudes continued to dictate that the nobility were the natural intermediaries between the king and the provinces. If a noble presence was lacking, then the gentry themselves were just as likely to provide leaders who might act as surrogate lords in the region: witness, for instance, the role of the Stanleys in the north-west under Richard II and Henry IV.[32] In assessing the political influence of the baronial affinity it is therefore largely fruitless to run through all the case studies undertaken in recent years and try to argue whether examples of independent gentry communities such as fourteenth-century Gloucestershire (itself a somewhat marginal case) and fifteenth-century Derbyshire were more 'typical' than those societies supposedly dominated by bastard feudalism, such as late fourteenth-century Devon or early fifteenth-century Warwickshire.[33] The really important question to ask is how, where they existed, baronial affinities were used to exert an influence on the political life both of the locality and, in some circumstances, of the realm as a whole. This in turn begs important questions about the role of the nobility in local, regional and national politics. For present purposes, we may identify three subjects for further analysis: the maintenance of peace in the localities; the control of local office-holding; and the influence of baronial retinues in the parliamentary commons.

Despite the remarkable growth of royal justice, it is clear that the ultimate guarantee of social stability and political peace in the later Middle Ages remained rooted in the conventions of lordship.

Such notions certainly help, for instance, to explain why, when the permanent commissions of the peace began to emerge in the fourteenth century, members of the peerage were appointed, wherever appropriate, as presidents of the county bench. But whereas their position in the courts was largely honorific, the nobility played a vital and active part in maintaining the system of dispute settlement that continued to operate outside the structure of royal justice in the later Middle Ages through the process of arbitration.[34] Recent studies have indicated that the endless wranglings over property that are such a feature of gentry society in this period were most effectively resolved by agreements imposed on the rival parties in what would now be called out of court settlements. Arbitration could be provided by anyone with sufficient status to command the deference essential to guarantee the resulting accord; but whereas churchmen largely controlled the system until the mid-fourteenth century, secular lords seem to have been much more frequently involved thereafter. Providing arbitration as a local public service probably became an increasingly important means of upholding the practical, as well as the merely symbolic, authority of the high aristocracy at a time when posts in the shire administration were coming to be controlled almost exclusively by the gentry. Furthermore, those seeking and securing such services were almost bound to be drawn into the influence, if not the retinue, of a great lord: both the even-handedness of his judgments and the authority to make them hold were the very attributes most likely to increase his political following. Arbitration thus became the essential means by which the affinity was both created and maintained. It also follows that lordship was regarded as one of the fundamental guarantees of stability. It is no accident that it was as arbitrators that major lords were often able to intervene in otherwise largely independent gentry societies: witness, for instance, the role of Ralph, Lord Cromwell, in mid-fifteenth-century Nottinghamshire.[35] And by the same token, the sudden removal of the dynasty or individual lord that had provided this essential point of reference could produce a severe crisis of confidence. The death of Richard Beauchamp, earl of Warwick, in 1439, followed by the minority and early death of his son, not only created a power vacuum in the Beauchamps' own counties of Worcestershire and Warwickshire but also necessitated a considerable re-adjustment of political lordship in the neighbouring regions of Staffordshire, Leicestershire, Northamptonshire and Gloucestershire.[36] It was not only the crown, but many county communities, that clearly looked to the high aristocracy as the natural guarantors of peace in the localities.

The late medieval nobility actually had surprisingly few formal responsibilities in local government: this, indeed, is one of the things that distinguishes them from their Norman predecessors and Tudor successors. Precisely because they did not act under royal commission, however, noblemen obviously expected the agencies of the state to be amenable to their will and, where possible, controlled by their own men. This convention in itself exemplified the symbiotic relationship between retainer and lord: the client benefited from admission to the pool of royal patronage, while the patron won general respect for the effectiveness of his lordship and gained direct influence over the workings of government. It has often been assumed that the nobility were thus able to take over the structure of local government and use it as a cover for their own, and their retainers', nefarious practices; taken to its natural conclusion, this means that clientage became not simply a form of social and political organisation but a means of subverting public authority and preventing the growth of a centralised state.[37] In fact, the degree of magnate control over royal office-holders was not usually so great as to allow for such a take-over: even the local political machinations of the Despensers under Edward II and of the duke of Suffolk under Henry VI depended only partly on their ability to manipulate the royal council into making the 'right' appointments in the shires.[38] In most cases, the nobility exercised neither the monopoly of influence at court nor the total domination over the gentry to allow for much more than occasional and relatively discreet interventions in the course of local government. This is highlighted by the case of John of Gaunt, who enjoyed not simply general influence but direct control over much of the administrative structure of the palatinate of Lancaster, but whose own retainers never had more than a partial monopoly of office-holding there and whose personal initiatives were sufficiently sporadic to create the need for a more decisive, rather than a less oppressive, exercise of lordship.[39] This example also reminds us that the nobility had more than mere local politics to concern them: Gaunt clearly regarded his responsibilities in the English provinces (particularly such a far-flung province as Lancashire) as of rather less significance than his roles on the national and international stages. Consequently, it may be that the true significance of the baronial affinity lies less in the hierarchical political structures it appears to represent than in the way it reinforced the existing collective identities within local gentry societies.

The local office most obviously open to magnate influence was also the one that provided the link between the shire communities and the central government: that of MP. There is clear evidence that members of the nobility attempted from time to time to secure the return of their own men as knights of the shire in parliament. But there is also much to indicate that the 'labouring' of elections (as such a practice was known) was increasingly less tolerated. Much of the complaint underlying individual cases of election-rigging in the early fourteenth century, and the campaign launched by the parliamentary commons in the Lancastrian period to ensure free elections and fair practice in the county courts, arose from suspicion of the sheriffs, rather than the magnates: the fact that the former might be acting as agents of the latter was only usually inferred.[40] In more sensitive circumstances, however, the influence of the nobles – and, indeed, of the crown – was identified and criticised more specifically, not least because it provided a possible means of excusing the apparent failure of the parliamentary commons to oppose controversial government policies. John of Gaunt was accused particularly of packing the parliament of January 1377, when the acts of the Good Parliament were overturned, and Richard II was accused at his deposition of interfering in elections to the parliament of September 1397 in order to extract taxes from the commons.[41] Finally, the complaint of the Kentish rebels of 1450 that 'the people may not have their free election in choosing knights of the shire' was a clear, if not actually explicit, reference to the way in which the parliamentary representation of their county had been taken over and abused by the affinities of Henry VI and the duke of Suffolk.[42] In other words, then, the political societies and networks operating at the shire level were remarkably resistant to the idea that their own systems of representation should be subverted by either the crown or the nobility. If the natural order dictated a general deference to the wishes of the elite, the provincial gentry saw no reason why their only role in high politics should simply be to act as mouthpieces of their superiors. To be a lord's 'man' was not necessarily to be his placeman.

This review of the political identities and attitudes of the later medieval gentry suggests that although there was no single institution outside parliament capable of forming and articulating the agenda of the lesser aristocracy, there were many contexts in which provincial landed society was able to develop a collective response to issues of public concern. In particular, it has indicated that, despite the undoubted growth of bastard feudalism in the later fourteenth and fifteenth centuries, the gentry did not simply become the agents of the nobility but had the capacity to develop political programmes representative of their own particular interests. Two particular instances of this distinctive agenda are to be found in the campaign for the enforcement of the labour laws in the years after the Black Death and in the parliamentary criticisms of government in the aftermath of the Peasants' Revolt, both of which have been identified as being inspired and led specifically by the lesser landed classes.[43] Thus it was that, in the interstices between the public world of local government and the private world of the baronial affinity, between the horizontal associations represented by the county court and the vertical relationships established by the baronial affinity, there emerged a political community at once rooted in the local societies whence it sprang and conscious of its participation in the business of the state.

Centre and Locality: the Points of Contact

This chapter has argued that the local political structures devised and used by late medieval English society may in reality have been less oppositional and certainly less self-contained than is sometimes suggested by the historian's preoccupation with categories. In particular, it has indicated that while each community, from manor to shire, had its own political identity and concerns, the increasingly complex structure of royal government and the development, during the later thirteenth and early fourteenth centuries, of the representative element in parliament had the effect of breaking down some of the practical barriers that had earlier tended to separate the high politics of the court from the low politics of the localities. Above all, as we shall see in the following chapters, the further expansion in both the fiscal and the judicial structures of the state brought the monarchy into regular contact with a wider cross-section of provincial society than ever before. In the sense that politics represents the reactions of the king's subjects to the policies of his government, the years after 1290 produced not only more grounds for complaint but also more issues that were of regional and national, rather than of merely local, concern. Before we turn to those issues, however, it is necessary to understand a little more of the communication networks that created this new sense of political community and made it possible for provincial society to make common cause against the crown.

Much has been written in recent years about the formal information systems developed by the late medieval state. Under Edward I, and more particularly from Edward III's time, the monarchy made increasing efforts to convey to its subjects certain details of the policies and events that dominated the centre. There were two principal ways in which this was done: by issuing writs to the sheriffs ordering proclamations to be made in the county courts, markets and other public places; and by requesting the clergy to perform processions, say prayers and preach sermons on behalf of the state and its enterprises.[44] Much of this propaganda – particularly that undertaken by the church – was designed to justify and popularise the wars against Scotland and France. But a significant proportion of the information disseminated by the crown's secular agents dealt with domestic business, above all with the conciliar ordinances and parliamentary statutes that created so much of the agenda of local government and politics. It is no surprise to find, then, that private petitioners even of peasant status also began in this period to cite royal and parliamentary legislation back at the king. While such petitions were presumably drafted not by the suitors but by reasonably well-informed lawyers operating in local courts, they nevertheless provide striking evidence of the way in which provincial society quickly adapted the crown's information system to its own advantage.[45] Political communication was clearly a two-way process.

Alongside these official mechanisms, there were many other more informal channels through which the details of high politics percolated into local society and influenced public perceptions of the state. Literary sources are of particular relevance and interest here. The chronicles of the fourteenth and fifteenth centuries, at least some of which, like the *Brut*, were fairly widely disseminated among the book-owning and literate classes, were of course very largely constructed around a high political narrative. It is especially interesting to notice what a prominent place was given to the central political assembly of parliament in the chronicles: in particular, there survive a number of extended eye-witness accounts of the more dramatic parliamentary sessions of the fourteenth century – those of 1321, 1341, 1376 and 1388 – preserved within larger chronicles or as free-standing narratives.[46] Perhaps more relevant in the present context, however, is the range of polemical literature – mostly poetry – that survives from the later Middle Ages. This material, still written in Anglo-Norman French at the start of the fourteenth century but increasingly thereafter in Middle English, is inevitably rather difficult to interpret: the sophistication of some of the ideas and forms employed indicates a relatively well-informed and educated authorship, while the very use of the written word raises questions as to whether this material can ever really be seen as truly representative of 'popular' politics. Ideally, one would wish to draw a distinction between political poems written in the provinces, which might indicate the types of information and ideas percolating down from the centre, and those composed near the court and circulated through the emerging London book market – material which could itself therefore provide local society with information about the course of high politics. Given that many of the texts are anonymous, this distinction cannot always easily be made.[47] But it is also pertinent to note that both categories of complaint literature often proceed from a markedly anti-establishment viewpoint, and both therefore provide us with something of a medieval worm's-eye view of royal government.

The emergence and flowering of this genre during the early fourteenth century has itself been taken to signify both the increased political awareness and, in many cases, the increased political disillusionment of the lower orders of English society.[48] The most eloquent expressions of that disillusionment, however, inevitably belong to the period after the Black Death and derive from that most widely circulated of political poems, William Langland's *Piers Plowman*. There is much debate as to Langland's own dependence on contemporary high politics for his subject matter. Was the figure of Lady Meed, for example, a caricature of Edward III's mistress Alice Perrers or simply a personification of the sin of venality? Similarly, did Langland's representation of parliament as a high court rather than as a political assembly reflect his (and, by implication, others') ignorance of the world of government, or was it intended to conflict deliberately with reality in order to demonstrate the desperate need felt in the 1370s for a monarchy that would once more take command of the institutions of the state?[49] Whatever the case, it is clear that those anonymous (probably London-based) writers who followed in Langland's tradition had no doubts about the details of high politics and no qualms about satirising them. Two apparently independent poems dating from *c.* 1400, *On King Richard's Ministers* and *Richard the Redeless*, both indulge in elaborate word-play on the names of Richard II's courtiers, John Bushey, Henry Green, William Bagot and William Scrope – a coincidence that may suggest the circulation of oral parodies of the royal household in the 1390s.[50] Certainly, the use of royal and aristocratic badges in the latter work to describe the way in which Richard (the hart) took vengeance on the Lords Appellant, Arundel (the horse), Gloucester (the swan) and Warwick (the bear) reflects the contemporary public controversy surrounding the impact of bastard feudalism. Most striking of all, however, is the pen-portrait of a parliamentary session provided in *Richard the Redeless*, where the commons are characterised as representatives not so much of their constituencies as of the frailty and corruption that the author clearly believed to pervade the whole political system.[51] This and other similar literary material therefore suggests an intriguing tension between the growing sense of frustration and alienation felt by those sections of society without direct access to the world of high politics and the continued fascination demonstrated by the same people in the actions of their superiors and the affairs of state.

The most interesting resolution of this tension, found in much of the literature of the fourteenth and fifteenth centuries, was an idealised image of a polity controlled not by the ministers or the magnates (both of which groups were dismissed as being essentially self-serving) but by a wider and more disparate public opinion represented by what contemporaries normally called 'the commons'. It is somewhat difficult to discern what this term really meant: not, in this context, the lower house of parliament; nor, apparently, the totality of the king's subjects (the Peasants' Revolt largely discredited any tendency towards the comprehensive application of the term, at least in the mind of William Langland);[52] but, instead, a concept that would later gain more coherence and clarity through the use of the phrases 'common weal' and 'commonwealth' and be used to describe both the broad political community and the general benefits that its rule bestowed.[53] In a poem of the late fourteenth century now usually entitled *On the Death of Edward III*, the conventional imagery of the ship of state is given originality and interest by the elaboration of the metaphor: the rudder was 'Edward the third, the noble knight' (whose removal the poem bemoans); the ship itself was 'the chivalry of this land'; but the mast, which ultimately dictated the direction of the vessel, was the 'good commons'.[54] The same theme was picked up by an anonymous preacher in Henry V's time: for him, the king was the master mariner, the clergy and nobility the fore- and aft-castles, and the people the hull.[55] These representations of national unity and the inclusive definition of the polity that they implied provide the most powerful evidence yet cited for the existence of a political community at the national level, as well as the merely provincial and local levels, in late medieval England.

4

Political Issues: Kingship

If there was one political issue on which almost everyone living in late medieval England may be assumed to have had some opinion, it was kingship. The problem for the historian is therefore very much the same as that which confronted the rulers of the fourteenth and fifteenth centuries: namely, to decide which of the many paradigms of medieval monarchy might be most fruitfully pursued. The modern tradition of historical biography tends to concentrate on the rise of administrative kingship and to assess the success or failure of later medieval rulers not so much on the basis of their great deeds as on the degree of commitment they demonstrated to the often mundane business of government. In one sense, of course, there is no doubt that the king's role as governor and political manager was crucial to the stability and popularity of his regime. The disadvantage of the modern tendency towards objective analysis and quantification, however, is that it tends to omit the mystique that surrounded medieval monarchy and the fact that a large proportion of the king's subjects judged him on often very subjective criteria. Although most of this chapter will be taken up with the development of a more sophisticated theory of kingship among the politically active classes during the fourteenth and fifteenth centuries and the resulting challenge this posed to the Plantagenet dynasty, it is as well to highlight the continued existence of older and more simplistic notions of monarchy by beginning our review of contemporary ideas on kingship with a summary of what might be called the popular view.

Ideas on Kingship

The essence of this popular view has to be extracted from the political literature written outside the immediate context of the schools, the court and the central government. Here, the discourse upon kingship, whether found in historical, prophetic, satirical or subversive writing, is characterised by three particular features. To begin with, there is a stark contrast between 'good kings' and 'bad kings', with few half measures or qualifications. Secondly, there is a strong emphasis on the historical and mythological past and the assessment of each ruler by direct comparison with his predecessors. Finally, there is a great deal of emphasis placed on heroic deeds in arms. These preoccupations are nicely summarised by the following extract from an obscure fifteenth-century Lincolnshire chronicle.

> In the year of our Lord, 1377, the magnificent King Edward [III] of Windsor, bearing in his bosom the uprightness of Hercules, the severity of Achilles, the moderation of Nestor, the courage of Ajax, the boldness of Theseus, after he had defended the kingdom of England on all sides from enemies, and manfully suppressed the pride of the Welsh and Scots, paid the debt of death in the fifty-first year of his reign. In the same year, Richard [II] of Bordeaux, son of Edward of Woodstock, [was] elected and crowned king. And he immediately, after the manner of Rehoboam, despising the counsel of the wise, attended to the suggestions of the young. Infatuated by their persuasions he oppressed his native subjects, and while he beggared them with his great exactions he enriched ignoble foreigners, to his own ruin, as afterwards it plainly appeared.[1]

Beneath this ostentatious display of classical learning lies a notably unsubtle interpretation of kingship and an obvious ignorance of certain facts. Ironically, for example, Edward III had himself been accused of acting like another Rehoboam (itself a fairly traditional charge against young kings) during his quarrel with Archbishop Stratford in 1340–1;[2] clearly, however, his subsequent record in arms made him more or less impervious to personal criticism at least in the popular historical tradition. It is also notable that although the articles of deposition of 1399 accused Richard II of promoting 'unworthy persons', there was no suggestion that he had favoured aliens;[3] rather than looking for possible targets among the Ricardian nobility, it is probably more realistic to see our chronicler's criticism as a conventional charge against all bad kings and one that had been given new life as a result of Henry III and Edward II's prominent friendships with 'foreigners'.

The degree to which the popular view of kingship was at variance with the reality of high politics can, however, be exaggerated. The political literature discussed here tended to present the king as an isolated figure and either failed to acknowledge or seriously under-rated the bureaucratic paraphernalia that increasingly surrounded the throne during the later Middle Ages. Yet the events in London and Westminster during the Peasants' Revolt of 1381 leave little doubt that the lower orders were highly conscious of the apparatus of government, the need to protect the king from the invidious influence of evil councillors, and the responsibility of the ruler to cut through the administrative conventions of the state by asserting his personal will. The most powerful political image of 1381, encapsulated in the demand for an end to all lordship save that of the king, can in some respects certainly be seen as a mark of the naivety of the rebels, who mistakenly assumed that the young Richard II would act as their champion. In another sense, however, it referred back to the theory and practice of unitary lordship – what we would call sovereignty – developed by Edward I at the end of the thirteenth century, which saw the crown not only as the source of all authority but also as the protector and guarantor of the rights of all its subjects.[4] In many respects, indeed, the popular image of the king as a solitary figure embodying the attributes of the state and imposing his personality on the government of the realm – an image exemplified in Richard II's time by *Piers Plowman* and in Henry V's by *The Crowned King* – was not so far removed from more sophisticated notions of monarchy developed in late medieval England.[5]

In attempting to reconstruct the attitudes of the elite – and, indeed, of the royal family itself – to this subject, we are able to draw on a more diverse body of evidence including not only the political literature of the court but also scholastic writing, administrative records and artistic images. At the heart of the courtly, as of the popular, image of kingship, of course, was the tradition of militant monarchy. Through their wars in Scotland and France, Edward I and Edward III became, both for their contemporaries and for posterity, the very exemplars of warrior kingship. In particular, they associated themselves with the potent figure of Arthur and presented both their victories in the field and their successful domestic regimes as the due rewards that accrued from divine favour. The impact can be seen in Richard II's reign, when, although the Chandos Herald's *Life of the Black Prince* and the continued royal patronage of tournaments helped to sustain courtly traditions of chivalry, the king's own manifest failure in arms and his personal propensity for peace inevitably came to be seen as a kind of betrayal of his office. It was therefore left to Henry V to restore and further enhance the tradition of the warrior king and to develop an even closer association between military success and divine favour: it is worth pointing out that, had it not been for the Reformation, Henry would probably have been remembered as much for the defence of orthodoxy and the slaying of heretics as for his victory against the French at Agincourt.

Despite the enduring appeal of the martial tradition, however, the later fourteenth and fifteenth centuries also witnessed the development of a new and more sophisticated view of monarchy which placed much greater emphasis on the responsibilities of the king in domestic government. To a limited extent, this can be put down to the influence of political theory. Giles of Rome's *The Rule of Princes*, written in the late thirteenth century, found its way into a number of royal and aristocratic, as well as scholarly, book collections in fourteenth-century England and helped to spawn a genre largely new to this country, namely the 'mirrors for princes' or 'letters to kings' dedicated to a series of English rulers from Edward III onwards.[6] On the other hand, the increasing range and complexity of the issues dealt with in these texts suggests that their authors were also very much influenced by the realities of political life. Alongside the traditional duties of defending the realm and the church and upholding justice, the mirrors of the late fourteenth and fifteenth centuries placed increasing stress on the king's role in providing 'good governance' through consultation with his wise men, diligent attention to the business of state, and in particular (a notable new emphasis here) the sound management of his resources. John Gower's ideas on monarchy, formulated under Richard II and Henry IV, and Thomas Hoccleve's *Regement of Princes*, addressed to the future Henry V, therefore provide a much more highly developed theory of kingship than that given by Walter Milemete's *The Nobility, Wisdom and Prudence of Kings*, written nearly a century earlier for the young Edward III. The main effect of this new theory was to give renewed importance to the leadership, legitimacy and authority vested in the king and to stress not the power but the responsibility that these functions bestowed. According to this tradition, monarchy was ultimately justified not by its sanctity but by its utility.

Such ideas did not chime well with the high view of kingship espoused by certain members of the Plantagenet dynasty. The growth of royal government in the thirteenth century had been accompanied by a new concern for the public imagery of the monarchy specifically intended to promote the sacred nature of the royal office. The foundation or re-building of major ecclesiastical establishments – Westminster Abbey by Henry III and Richard II, Vale Royal by Edward I, Sheen and Syon by Henry V, Eton and King's College, Cambridge, by Henry VI – was simply a continuation of an older tradition of royal commemoration. But the later Middle Ages also witnessed the revival or adoption of an increasingly wide range of media through which the royal image was promoted: the royal castles and palaces of Caernarfon, Westminster and Windsor, the Eleanor Crosses, the royal tombs with their new emphasis on portraiture, the numerous sculptural galleries of kings (still extant on the choir screens at Canterbury and York and in Richard II's great hall at Westminster) and the iconography of the seals and gold coinages of Edward III and Henry VI all provide striking evidence of a new campaign to promote the monarchy and, in particular, to emphasise its divinity.[7] For the modern historian, the most striking and bizarre manifestation of this process is the royal touch, the practice first adopted in England by Henry III and Edward I whereby the king claimed to be able to heal those suffering from scrofula merely by the laying on of hands or making the sign of the cross. To those already disposed towards the idea, the royal touch evidently provided dramatic evidence that the true source of the king's authority lay not on earth but in heaven.[8]

It is not surprising, then, that those kings who lacked real and practical proof of divine favour in the form of military victories increasingly fell back on the symbolic and ceremonial aspects of kingship and attempted to justify their more controversial policies by claiming that they were answerable only to God. In particular, Richard II's tendencies towards what has rather anachronistically been called 'absolutism' were accompanied not only by the commissioning of major artistic and architectural statements of monarchical supremacy but also by a rather unlikely campaign to secure Edward II's canonisation as a royal martyr.[9] To see Richard's deposition as a triumph for the 'political' over the 'royal' approach to kingship, however, need not lead us back to the discredited nineteenth-century notion that the subsequent Lancastrian regime was a 'parliamentary' or 'constitutional' monarchy. Nor is it wise to assume that there was a continuous tension between the hieratic and the political models: just as most kings, for most of the time, recognised the need to seek the co-operation and consent of their subjects, so too was there a widespread assumption that good government depended on the exercise of the royal prerogative. It is significant that when, shortly after the close of our period, Sir John Fortescue attempted to distinguish between the constitutional practices of late medieval France and England, he described the latter not simply as a 'political' system, but as a *dominium politicum et regale* in which both polity *and* king had active and recognised parts to play.[10] Nevertheless, the fact that Fortescue conceived the constitution in this form and contrasted it so strongly with the *dominium regale* of France provides powerful evidence that those in the upper levels of political society had indeed resisted the notion of divine right and had come more and more to

perceive monarchy as a corporate and collaborative – in Fortescue's language a 'collegiate' – form of government.[11] In conceptual if not always in practical terms, the active engagement of the
polity in the life of the state was thus established.

The role of the king was so fundamental in the politics of late
medieval England that it is difficult to find any issue in which he
was not involved either directly or by association. In the present
chapter we shall concentrate our attention on political debates
surrounding the exercise of the royal will and the royal
prerogative, leaving to later treatment those categories of business
that depended less on the personality of the king and more on the
institution that we may call the crown. The distinction is inevitably
slightly artificial, but it does help to highlight the fact that the
course of late medieval politics was dictated both by the particular
abilities of individual rulers and by the evolving apparatus of the
state.

Political Management: Patronage

In shifting the focus away from those great constitutional set pieces
that so preoccupied nineteenth- and early twentieth-century historians, K. B. McFarlane and his disciples have found the key to
late medieval politics in the disposition of patronage and the public
debate this supposedly engendered. Although this revisionism is
itself currently being subjected to criticism and qualification,[12]
there can surely be little doubt that patronage in its widest and
broadest sense provided a natural preoccupation in a political
society built on and maintained by the patron–client relationship.
Patronage was the outward sign of good lordship, and the search
for good lordship, as we have seen, was an instinctive response in
medieval political society.

Royal patronage was extended to the political community in
two ways: directly, by the issue of grants of favour to individual
subjects; and indirectly, by the trickle-down effect that resulted

from the creation of new members of the nobility and their desire and need to demonstrate largesse to their own followers. Much patronage in the later Middle Ages was still dispensed in the latter fashion. But it would be a great mistake to assume that kings were concerned only with the creation of the titled nobility. We have already noted in chapter 2 how the court, and particularly the chamber, had by the end of our period become a particular focus for those seeking access to the king's grace, and how the affinities of Richard II and the house of Lancaster created a powerful group of royal beneficiaries among the provincial gentry. Before proceeding to the political debates surrounding this issue, then, it is as well to emphasise the sheer range of the crown's activities by beginning at the lower end and working up through the scale of patronage.

Much of the minor patronage dispensed by the crown during the later Middle Ages was reactive, responding directly to petitions from individual subjects. Although many of the favours thus requested could be resolved routinely and were simply channelled through the council into the relevant government departments, there remained a very substantial number of petitions which were judged matters *de gratia* (of grace) and could be decided only by the king in person. The amount of such business is rather difficult to judge, but it seems almost certain that there was a substantial increase across our period: Edward III probably had to deal in person with several hundred requests a year, whereas Henry IV's annual turnover of petitions was at least 2,000 and may have been as high as 4,000.[13] This does not mean, of course, that the resources on which the king had to draw were necessarily greater or that the actual amount of minor patronage dispensed by the crown increased in direct proportion to demand; it is simply a reflection of the fact that the king's subjects were taking a considerably more direct approach towards securing their own share of royal favour. On the other hand, it should be noted that while some sources of minor patronage undoubtedly dwindled during the later Middle Ages (custodies of vacant feudal escheats, for example, declined in value and number as a result of adverse economic circumstances and the crown's willingness to allow such estates to be administered by trusts), many others did indeed expand to meet demand. The number of ecclesiastical benefices in the king's gift increased approximately five-fold in the course of the first half of the fourteenth century as a result of a deliberate policy of expropriation designed to benefit the growing army of royal clerks in the central administration.[14] Similarly, the number of new posts available in local government from the later thirteenth century, and the marked expansion in the size both of the tax commissions and of the peace commissions appointed at shire level during the fourteenth and fifteenth centuries, suggests that the crown was seeking to gratify the administrative, political and social aspirations of a growing number of the shire gentry as the period progressed. Finally, the marked increase from Richard II's time in the number of fees and annuities paid out of the exchequer (and in particular, after 1399, from the resources of the duchy of Lancaster) in order to maintain the king's affinity provides the most obvious indication of the broader scope, as well as the burden, of royal patronage in this period. It is as well perhaps to remember that this financial burden, and the resulting complaints analysed below, arose not simply from the overweening political ambitions of a Richard II or the outrageous extravagance of a Henry VI but also from an increase in the expectations and demands of the king's own subjects.

The attitude of the high nobility to the major patronage dispensed in the form of titles and land settlements was similarly double-edged, in that it assumed the king's responsibility regularly to re-stock the ranks of the peerage while also remaining deeply resistant to the newcomers on whom the king's favour so often focused. At the beginning of our period, in 1311, the aristocratic opposition to Edward II actually attempted to encroach on the king's freedom of action by requiring that major patronage be dispensed only in parliament and with the consent of the baronage.[15] This was probably intended for a specific purpose, to prevent the rise of another Gaveston. However, it also enshrined an informal political convention which survived the abolition of the Ordinances and was generally observed even by the likes of Richard II, whereby the creation or revival of noble titles was expected to take place on those occasions when the king had the high aristocracy assembled about him: it is even possible that two of the titles bestowed by Richard outside this usual context, during the Scottish campaign of 1385, were successfully vetoed by the lords when parliament assembled at Westminster later in the same year.[16] To the nobility at least, then, there was little doubt that major royal patronage was a legitimate subject for political debate.

This aristocratic tradition of participation in the disposition of patronage became all the more important as a result of two interconnected developments in the later Middle Ages: the emergence of a new and more elaborate scale of honours, which introduced the ranks of duke and marquis (in the fourteenth century) and viscount (in the fifteenth) into the peerage alongside those of earl and baron; and the integration of an increasing number of cadet branches of the royal family into the English nobility. Although Edward III and Henry V may have entertained hopes of settling their sons (in the first case) and brothers (in the second) in the outposts of their newly-enlarged empires, both kings also observed the convention that the princes of the blood should enjoy special marks of status within England.[17] The title of duke was first adopted in 1337 specifically for this purpose, and was still considered as the natural preserve of the royal family in the mid-fifteenth century: Henry VI's elevation of both John and Edmund Beaufort to the dukedom of Somerset and his creations of John Holland and Humphrey Stafford as dukes of Exeter and Buckingham during the 1440s could all be seen as due signs of favour to descendants of the younger sons of Edward III, and especially necessary for forging dynastic solidarity at a time when Henry himself lacked a direct heir.[18] By the same token, however, Richard II was much criticised for the way in which he corrupted the rank of duke by bestowing it on Robert de Vere in 1386 and on a whole group of his followers – the *duketti*, or little dukes, as one chronicler disparagingly referred to them – in 1397, while Henry VI's promotion of William de la Pole from earl to marquis and then to duke of Suffolk did much to jeopardise what sense of political cohesion still existed among the royal dukes in the 1440s.[19] The tension between insiders and outsiders which had always been at the root of the political debate over major patronage was therefore greatly intensified as a result of the extraordinarily complex web of family relationships that grew up between the crown and the aristocracy in the later Middle Ages.

To what extent was the nobility's preoccupation with royal patronage shared by the wider political community? It is not surprising that those outside the peerage should have showed a sympathy with the ideas of their superiors. Thus, for example, the sentiments expressed by Bishop Brinton of Rochester in the Good Parliament of 1376 and by the rebels of Kent during Cade's Rebellion of 1450 demonstrate a general allegiance to the aristocratic assumption that the princes and nobles of the blood should form a kind of super-aristocracy capable of playing a dominant role in the affairs of state.[20] More interestingly, however, the interests represented in the parliamentary commons appear to have begun to develop their own concerns and programmes of reform during the later fourteenth and fifteenth centuries, concentrating not so much on the political repercussions of major patronage (which tended to be most evident within the relatively closed confines of the court and council) but on the more obvious *financial* consequences arising from the alienation of royal rights and resources at all levels in the system of patronage.[21] The fact that members of the commons were themselves among the principal beneficiaries of the lower levels of crown patronage simply serves to remind us of the particular sensitivity and relevance of this debate both to them and to their constituents.

What sparked off this more general concern over royal patronage was the escalation in the expenditure of the royal household – including, from Richard II's reign, the added cost of the royal affinity – and the very notable reluctance of parliament to accept responsibility for the royal debts that resulted. From the time of the Good Parliament, the commons began to argue that the distribution of *all* forms of patronage, from the greatest noble estate to the meanest feudal escheat, was potentially compromising to the financial security of the crown and, by extension, imposed unnecessary and arguably illegitimate burdens on its subjects. By the 1390s the crown was clearly attempting to extend the circumstances under which it might demand extraordinary taxes; but although the commons were prepared to make discretionary grants in the king's favour on a number of occasions under Henry IV and Henry VI, they almost always used the opportunity to set terms, requiring the parliamentary audit of tax accounts, demanding economies and/or priorities in the pattern of household spending and insisting on the reservation of traditional revenues so that ordinary expenditure was supported as much as possible out of ordinary income. The final and most drastic measure, proposed in 1404–6 and actually implemented, with many qualifications and exemptions, in 1450–1, was an act of resumption, by which all lands and other forms of profit granted away in patronage over a specified period of time were taken back into the direct control of the crown and used to subsidise the costs of the household and affinity.

The general reluctance of the commons to assume responsibility for the upkeep of the court was based less on a naive belief that the king had infinite resources of wealth at his disposal (the statements of income and expenditure presented to them on occasion from the 1360s were enough to put this particular myth to rest) but on their own very traditional view of the distinction between the public and private faces of the monarchy. Parliamentary taxation ought, above all, to be reserved for the costs of war. Outside this sphere, the king should not presume to ask for assistance; and if he did so, then he had to accept that the special obligations of his subjects did not obtain and that the conditions they set might be a good deal more stringent. (The clergy in convocation, though sometimes lacking the political unity or will to withstand the considerable pressure brought to bear by the crown for tax grants, also held by the same basic principle.)[22] In the present context, however, the most striking thing about the build-up to the parliamentary demands for resumption is the way in which the disposition of patronage – so often regarded by historians as the essence of the royal prerogative – had become hedged about with a series of formal and informal restrictions imposed not simply by the peerage but by the provincial power elites represented in the parliamentary commons. Royal patronage had indeed become the business of the polity.

Political Management: the King and the Law

If the king's freedom to dispense patronage was a growing cause of public concern during the later Middle Ages, how did his other prerogative powers fare in the face of more concerted and sophisticated political debate? The other obvious area in which the will of the ruler imposed itself on the government of the realm was in the making, interpretation and implementation of the law. The actual judicial structures and the more general public debate on justice will be discussed in chapter 6; here we are concerned with the attitudes of individual rulers and the responses they provoked among the political community. Three subjects in particular beg our attention: the king's control over legislation; his role as arbitrator in disputes between members of the nobility; and his approach to the punishment of political opponents.

In the Middle Ages, scholastic discussions of the relationship between the king and the law drew an important distinction between divine or natural law and human law: that is, between the rightful and immutable customs by which society was regulated and the principles laid down by rulers and their legal advisers for the better government of the state.[23] Whereas the king had no right to breach divine law, there were some who argued that he ought to be placed above human law in order to act as a check on the fallibility of earthly institutions and ensure that only good and just laws were enforced. In England, this already ambiguous situation was complicated by the absence of a written law code, the association between the common law and natural law, and the assumption that the body of statutory legislation which began to grow so markedly from the time of Edward I was only valid so long as it was compatible with common law principles. To overthrow a statute founded in the common law was therefore, in some senses, to confront natural law and offend the will of God. This, coupled with the early development of English political institutions, helps to explain why the exercise of the royal prerogative was such an extraordinarily sensitive issue throughout our period.

In 1308 the coronation oath was altered and Edward II was required not only to 'grant and preserve ... the laws and customs granted ... by former kings of England' but also to 'hold and preserve the laws and righteous customs which the community of [the] realm shall have chosen': in other words, to guarantee the integrity of both past and future legislation.[24] The significance of these oaths has been played down by most twentieth-century historians, partly because in 1308 the phrase 'community of the realm' was still usually applied to the baronage rather than to the wider polity represented in parliament, and partly because the clause may have been intended only for a specific purpose, to secure the re-adoption of Edward I's Confirmation of the Charters and Articles upon the Charters. Furthermore, the qualification about '*righteous* customs' (my italics) clearly provided both Edward II and his successors in 1322, 1341 and 1387 with a convenient excuse for condemning and annulling legislation forced upon them against their will and infringing what they regarded as their innate prerogative powers.[25] That said, it is also clear that the polity remained deeply committed to the idea that the king should be guided and constrained by the law. Both Edward II and Richard II were accused at the time of their depositions of abusing the law for their own political ends, and, in Richard's case, of making it up as he went along: in the memorable and probably over-dramatic words of the deposition articles, that he 'frequently replied and declared expressly, with an austere and determined expression, that the laws were in his mouth, or, at other times, that they were in his breast'.[26] The inference – that those kings who abused the basic principles of justice enshrined in natural law lost their claim to legitimate authority – was certainly not lost on Richard's immediate successors. In 1401 when the commons affirmed the existence of the prerogative by declaring Henry IV to be 'in as great liberty as his noble ancestors before him', the king was quick to respond that 'it is not his intention nor his will to change the laws, statutes or good customs . . . but to keep the ancient laws and statutes ordained and used in the time of his noble ancestors'. In other words, the prerogative, while remaining the acknowledged way in which the king protected his own rights and (as Henry IV himself put it in 1399) dispensed with laws 'which have been against the good purpose and common profit of the realm', could not rightfully challenge the due process of justice and the rule of law.[27] If England had a constitution in the later Middle Ages, it was surely grounded in this principle.

The second aspect of the king's personal involvement in the law relates to his role in preserving peace among the great lords of the realm. Major noblemen did not necessarily expect to have to take their disputes to the courts, not least because, when they did so, they often had to contend with each other's efforts to pervert the course of justice: witness what happened when the quarrel between Lord Cromwell and the duke of Exeter over the possession of the lordship of Ampthill was taken to litigation in the court of common pleas during the early 1450s.[28] But neither did they necessarily see violence as the first recourse or natural means of settling such matters. Wherever possible, in fact, the lords favoured the mechanism of mediation and looked naturally to the king to act as arbitrator. Much of the political stability that characterised the regimes of Edward III and Henry V can indeed be accounted for by the willingness of the aristocracy to accept the adjudications meted out in person by these most popular and respected monarchs.[29] By the same token, however, the withdrawal or blocking of the king's services or suspicion of royal partiality left the nobility in a very difficult position. In the 1320s, for example, those lords with grievances against the king's friends, the Despensers, had no option but to take up arms against them even though such actions were bound, in this context, to be construed as rebellion against the crown itself. The sentences of exile that Richard II imposed on *both* parties in the dispute between Henry Bolingbroke and the duke of Norfolk in 1398 gave obvious grounds both for personal and for more general political dissatisfaction with the king's ability to manage the high nobility. There is a somewhat fragmentary but undoubtedly seductive thesis that sees the origins of the Wars of the Roses in a series of private feuds between members of the nobility – Neville and Percy, Courtenay and Bonville, Lisle and Berkeley – during the middle years of the fifteenth century.[30] Whether or not the descent into civil war can be explained *solely* in these terms, it is clear that the lack of political integrity and the blatant favouritism demonstrated by Henry VI during his personal rule destroyed the respect and trust that was the necessary basis of successful dispute settlement. In terms of royal arbitration, then, the nobility clearly needed and sought not the curtailment of the crown's prerogative powers but the more effective exercise of such discretion as a means of promoting political harmony.

The third subject to be discussed here is the response of late medieval kings to those members of the nobility who rose in rebellion against them.[31] In one respect, the early years of our period witnessed a notable shift in attitudes to armed resistance that gave great advantage to the crown. Until the thirteenth century it was accepted that the feudal tenants in chief had the right – indeed, the duty – both to resist unreasonable actions by the king and, if necessary, to 'defy' him by renouncing their homage and raising war. Under Edward I, however, the concept of treason was extended to cover not only plotting the death of the king but also the act of armed rebellion, and although the statute of treasons of 1352 in many ways represented a political compromise between crown and nobility, it also enshrined this new principle and effectively nullified the older tradition of legitimate resistance. Clearly, the political stakes involved in rebellion were higher than ever before.

This development also, however, raised emotive questions among the aristocracy as to how the crown should conduct treason trials and treat convicted traitors. The arbitrary condemnations and executions imposed by Edward II in the aftermath of the battle of Boroughbridge represented a new brutality unknown even in the days of King John, and when Edward himself was deposed and murdered it was clear to both sides that a new accommodation had to be reached. The result took two principle forms. First, the crown largely abandoned the practice of judgment by notoriety and normally allowed treason trials to proceed by due judicial process at common law: this explains why Richard II's use of the prerogative court of chivalry as a means of disposing of his political enemies was specifically condemned in 1399.[32] Secondly, and perhaps more significantly, the crown commonly mitigated the otherwise ferocious penalties of treason. The statute of treasons had restricted the types of lands that were liable to forfeiture from condemned traitors by implicitly excluding those that were entailed or held in trust. But in 1398 these restrictions were lifted so that the surviving relatives of the offender could, in theory, lose everything, and under Henry IV the crown began to apply the legal doctrine of corruption of blood to implicate the traitor's heirs in his own offence. The aristocracy was probably persuaded to accept the increasing severity of these penalties because it knew that one of the king's primary responsibilities was to temper justice with mercy. The political restoration of the Despenser and Mortimer families by Edward III or of the Percys, Montagues and Despensers (again) by Henry V was therefore a demonstration not of political weakness but of the king's primary duty to promote stability and concord throughout the realm. Thus, while the free exercise of the royal will was no longer tolerated in the condemnation and disposal of traitors, the royal prerogative remained the essential instrument of political rehabilitation and reconciliation. How much more important it was, then, that the prerogative should be wisely and justly exercised.

This discussion of the king's role in relation to the law tends to suggest that there was always something of a tension between the power of the monarchy and the personal interests of its principal subjects: the nobles liked the prerogative when it suited them, but encouraged the polity to condemn it when it did not. This is not to imply, however, that crown and nobility were locked in some kind of continuous struggle for power. Indeed, most kings recognised that, since they lacked the coercive power necessary to rule completely by will, there was little point in developing a theory of royal supremacy or adopting a confrontational approach to government. It was only when they lost touch with those realities that Edward II, Richard II and Henry VI had to face concerted resistance and, ultimately, defeat. To understand the significance of those defeats we shall conclude this chapter with a discussion of the most striking of all political acts in this period, the forcible removal of kings.

Royal Depositions

The historian who seeks to understand the impact of royal depositions on the political system of later medieval England has to resist the temptation of turning a sequence of isolated events into a coherent story and writing in terms of a 'series' of depositions carried out between 1327 and 1485. Deposition was an aberration, and the idea that it might create a basis for future constitutional action was quite alien to kings and their subjects alike.[33] Consequently, although the dynastic disruptions of the later fifteenth century conventionally take on a certain historical coherence within the story of the Wars of the Roses, there is very little to suggest that the depositions of Edward II, Richard II and Henry VI followed any consistent pattern or set particular precedents for the future. The following discussion of those earlier depositions therefore sets them in deliberate opposition in order to highlight both the contrasting procedures by which they were effected and their relative impact on the political life of the realm.

Although medieval political thought justified resistance against tyrannical regimes, there were no clear scholastic arguments condoning the forcible removal of a legitimately ordained (and, in the English case, anointed) king. Nor was it really possible to develop a justification of deposition out of the interesting, though significantly isolated, argument put forward by a group of English barons in 1308 that they owed allegiance more to the institution of the crown than to the person of the king: claiming the right to constrain the king was tantamount to accroaching the royal power, an offence which both the crown and its opponents used in the fourteenth century arbitrarily to remove their political enemies.[34] Consequently, those who participated in the overthrow of Edward II's regime in the winter of 1326–7 had no clear precedent or legitimacy for their actions. The articles of deposition presented to the parliament of January 1327 provided general justification for Edward's removal by setting him in the tradition of the *rex inutilis*, the king who was 'useless' to his office, his regime and his subjects; it is even possible that these articles were modelled on a similar series of statements used to justify the deposition of Adolph of Nassau, king of the Romans, in 1298.[35] But it proved impossible to force the king to answer the accusations: indeed, the absence of a formal trial depriving him of authority either at this stage or following the transfer of power to Edward III was a serious constitutional deficiency only overcome in the most arbitrary way by the murder of the ex-king at Berkeley Castle later in 1327.[36] What legitimacy the procedures did have stemmed very largely from the formal deputation, representative of the estates of the realm, sent to the king at Kenilworth to announce the withdrawal of the allegiance and homage of his subjects and to receive from him a formal declaration of abdication.

From the general perspective of this book, it is particularly interesting to notice that the deposition of 1327 was brought about not by a palace revolution or even by the baronage acting in the name of the 'community of the realm', but in association with a full parliament containing representatives of the shires and towns and through the agency of a deputation of bishops, abbots, earls, barons, knights of the shires, barons of the Cinque Ports, Londoners and other townsmen, as well, possibly, as a group of friars.[37] It is therefore a striking example of the active involvement and symbolic importance of the broader political community in high politics. To go further and suggest that these events fundamentally altered the constitutional balance of the state is, however, seriously to misrepresent the politics of the fourteenth century. The unfortunate fate of Edward II is only known to have been cited in political dialogue with the crown on two occasions over the following seventy years: in 1341, during Edward III's quarrel with Archbishop Stratford; and in 1386, when Thomas of Woodstock and the bishop of Ely, acting as spokesmen for parliament, told Richard II that an 'ancient statute' (which did not actually exist) and 'recent example' (that is, the case of Edward II) provided them with justification for deposing him unless he agreed to the dismissal and impeachment of Michael de la Pole.[38] The contrasting reactions of the two kings are in themselves highly revealing. Edward III wisely refused to be drawn on the fate of his father and heard nothing more of the matter. But Richard II's refusal to co-operate with the commission set up in the Wonderful Parliament and his attempt to defeat his baronial opponents by force of arms at the battle of Radcot Bridge precipitated another threat of deposition in the winter of 1387–8 and even, according to one chronicler, a temporary withdrawal of allegiance by the Appellants and a discussion as to whether Henry of Bolingbroke or Thomas of Woodstock ought to be king.[39] Despite the fact that he survived this attempted coup, Richard remained highly sensitive to the challenge of deposition and spent some time in the 1390s ensuring that the precedent of 1327 was formally invalidated and could not be used against him.[40] Ironically, he seems to have been successful in this if in no other respect, for when his own deposition occurred in 1399 it was effected by a significantly different process.

In the period between his capture of Richard II at Conway and the opening of the parliament that would recognise his own kingship, Henry Bolingbroke set up a commission of academics and other churchmen to devise arguments and procedures for the transfer of royal power. It is interesting that the events of 1327 were avoided: instead, it was on the basis of the papal deposition of the Emperor Frederick II in 1245 that these canonists suggested Richard might legitimately be deprived of his title.[41] When the parliament opened, the estates were presented with a *fait accompli*: Richard had abdicated and Henry now claimed the throne (exactly on what basis still remains something of an issue). But again in contrast to 1327, Richard was now subjected to a series of charges which provided the basis for a formal sentence of deposition stripping him of any residual authority and leaving Bolingbroke free to establish himself as king. Many of the differences between 1327 and 1399 can be explained in terms of Richard II's lack of a direct heir and the search for a more legalistic settlement that would adequately justify Henry IV's coup. But the contrasts also provide a salutary reminder of the fact that the political community of later medieval England was much more inclined to seek means of resolving specific political crises than to develop new constitutional principles. In the absence of clear theoretical justification or legal precedent, the politics of crisis could only be pragmatic.

It has already been suggested in chapter 1 that the political revolts of the early fifteenth century suggest a certain contrast between the undisputed right of Edward III to rule as his father's heir and the more contentious and dubious nature of the Lancastrian claim to the throne. The extraordinary pressure that parliament was able to apply on the early regime of Henry IV in reference to the composition of the council and to the financing of the royal household also suggests that the polity was much more inclined to assert itself in the aftermath of the 1399 revolution. This, however, is a long way from suggesting that the fundamental constitutional structures had been altered or that the throne had passed into the gift of the political community. Indeed, the very ambiguity of the Lancastrians' dynastic claim made it in certain respects more difficult, and certainly more hazardous, to argue the case for deposition even in the face of that ultimate example of the *rex inutilis*, Henry VI. When Richard of York claimed the throne in 1460 the lords in parliament found it impossible to accept the argument that the true line of succession had been ignored and usurped in 1399: to do so would be to admit not only that the previous sixty years of Lancastrian rule had been illegitimate but also that the service provided and the patronage won by the landed and governing classes during that regime had all been invalid. The most they were prepared to do was to adopt the sort of compromise worked out in another context by the treaty of Troyes, allowing Henry VI's regime to run its course but recognising York, rather than the young prince of Wales, as the heir apparent. It was on the basis of this settlement, and on the judgment of God declared through victory in the field, that York's son was to pre-empt the formalities of deposition and have himself unilaterally declared and crowned king as Edward IV in 1461.[42] Once again, the realities of the moment prevented the use of precedent and illustrated the continued absence of any clear justification for the forcible removal of kings.

This brief analysis of the depositions of 1327, 1399 and 1461 indicates that there was no recognised system for removing incompetent kings in later medieval England and challenges the notion that the earlier episodes in the 'series' of late medieval depositions were accompanied by a necessary decline in either the theoretical or, indeed, the real *legitimate* powers of the monarchy. It is true that, even before 1461, foreigners were commenting on the English habit of overthrowing kings; John Lydgate's *Fall of Princes*, written in the 1430s, represents a domestic example of the same tendency to construct a consistent theme around otherwise quite separate events and give them some overall didactic purpose.[43] But in constitutional terms there is nothing to suggest that the forcible removal of Edward II, Richard II or Henry VI gave the polity any formal contractual control or veto over the individual who held the crown. In some ways, indeed, the three depositions discussed above appear to demonstrate constitutional *regression* as the role of the wider political community retreated from direct engagement in the transfer of power to a token and retrospective acknowledgement of the legitimacy of those who had already, by the act of conquest and usurpation, established themselves as *de facto* kings. It is hardly surprising, then, that when the frequency, and the arbitrariness, of such usurpations increased during the period we know as the Wars of the Roses, more and more people withdrew from active engagement in the struggle for power and sought to minimise the political and administrative disruption that inevitably threatened to accompany any change of regime.[44] This same desire for security and normality undoubtedly explains why the events of 1327 and 1399 played so little part in the political discourse or constitutional development of the fourteenth and early fifteenth centuries. Deposition signified the defeat of individual kings, not the debasement of monarchy.

The foregoing discussion has suggested that the success or failure of late medieval kingship is to be accounted for not simply by the personalities and achievements of individual rulers, vitally important though these were, nor through the analysis of constitutional crises such as royal depositions, which in some respects indeed can distort our wider understanding of contemporary attitudes to monarchy. Rather, it has aimed to demonstrate that, as a direct result of the development of political institutions and conventions during the fourteenth and fifteenth centuries, the exercise of royal power came more and more to be justified and judged in terms of its capacity to fulfil the expectations and demands of the polity. In some respects, this actually enhanced the king's power: the increasing dependence of the nobility on the exercise of the royal prerogative of pardon and the particularly striking growth in requests for the dispensation of royal patronage served to expand the amount of administrative and judicial business in which the ruler had a direct and personal responsibility. On the other hand, the over-use or abuse of the royal prerogative simply to enhance the king's authority or to silence his enemies was less and less tolerated as the political community came to expect and demand the observation of certain conventions: that the king act in accordance with the law, that he observe due process in the courts, that he dispense patronage widely and wisely while reserving sufficient of his own resources to meet ordinary expenditure. Much of what has been said here, however, relates directly to the relationship between the king and the very top levels of the political elite. That is inevitable in the sense that the royal will was expressed most frequently and properly in relation to the great men of the realm. It is time now to move on to the broader political issues that arose less from the personal actions of rulers and more from the priorities and demands of the state, and which impinged on the experiences not only of the aristocracy but of the generality of the king's subjects.

5

POLITICAL ISSUES: WAR

Among the many issues that arose in the political dialogue between crown and community during the fourteenth and the first half of the fifteenth centuries, two matters were of fundamental importance: the making of war, and the maintenance of justice. In certain respects, these priorities were nothing new. Since medieval society saw the king's primary responsibilities in terms of the defence of the realm from outside attack and the preservation of internal peace through the provision of good laws, the general concerns of the polity remained much the same under the Plantagenets as under the Norman and Angevin regimes. Nevertheless, the particular intensity of military activity between the 1290s and the 1450s, coupled with major changes in the structure of, and expectations placed upon, royal justice, meant that the debates surrounding these issues became more complex and lively than ever before. They therefore provide the obvious themes around which to base the following two chapters.

The other reason for selecting and then separating these two issues is that they are very often seen as having competed for priority in the business of the late medieval state. During the later thirteenth century Henry III and Edward I created (in the modern jargon) a 'law state' in which the authority of the crown and the justification of government rested principally in the exercise of jurisdiction and the guarantee of justice for all the king's free subjects. The outbreak of war with Scotland and France in the 1290s, and more particularly from the 1330s, supposedly switched the crown's attention from these matters and created a 'war state' in which the energies and resources of the central government were increasingly taken up in the task of servicing the military effort. According to this model of political development, the war state could not sustain the authoritarian ethos and centralising tendencies of the law state, but had to reach a compromise in which the king was guaranteed the parliamentary subsidies necessary to carry on the military effort and the county communities were accorded rights of self-government through the devolution of administrative and judicial responsibility to the landed elite.[1]

This thesis is picked up and discussed at various stages in the following two chapters. But it is important from the outset to appreciate that it rests on a number of assumptions challenged in this and certain other recent studies of later medieval England.[2] To begin with, the stark contrast between 'law state' and 'war state' can inevitably be over-drawn: the late medieval crown did not give up the judicial authority it developed in the thirteenth century, but merely implemented it in a different way. Secondly, as has already been suggested, the distinction between centre and locality can be overplayed in reference to a kingdom that was so conditioned to the experience of royal authority and which developed such a sophisticated system of representation at the national level: the idea that the county should be in charge of its own affairs arguably carried a good deal more political resonance in the thirteenth century, when the local communities had no effective voice in central politics, than it did in the fourteenth, when the parliamentary commons were capable of articulating issues of general concern to the entire realm.[3] Finally, the language we use and the judgements we make about the transfer from law state to war state can itself seriously distort the realities of the power structure. Because historians have customarily judged politics from the king's point of view, we still tend to think of centralisation as a mark of authority, and devolution as a sign of weakness; if devolution is also assumed to imply alienation or (to use a very modern term) privatisation, then the suspicion of royal 'failure' becomes still stronger. If, however, we accept that the late medieval state existed not simply in the sovereignty of the crown and the apparatus of central government but also in the power elites whose co-operation was so important to the effective implementation of royal policy, then the tension is largely resolved; indeed, the late Middle Ages can then be seen as a period in which the parameters of the state, far from receding, were notably and successfully extended. R. C. Palmer has recently characterised this process as a move from a government of 'innate authority', where power was based chiefly in private, feudal and seigneurial rights, to one of 'inherent authority', where provincial elites were accorded royal, public rights that allowed them to act directly as agents of the state.[4] This leaves one substantial question that will have to be addressed more fully in what follows: to what degree did this development create an oligarchical system of government and thus confound the influence of the broader political community identified and anatomised in earlier chapters? Whose interests were really served by the evolution of administrative, financial and judicial structures in the era of the Hundred Years War and the Black Death?

The chronological boundaries of this book and much of its sense of unity are dictated by the series of military engagements that historians have chosen to call the Hundred Years War. Perhaps 'long Hundred Years War' would be a better term to use, since it is now generally acknowledged that the Anglo-French struggles of the period fall into three phases stretching over a century and a half: the wars of the treaty of Paris from 1294 to 1360; the wars of the treaty of Brétigny from 1369 to 1420; and a war of the treaty of Troyes from 1420 to the final collapse of the English military presence in France in 1453. It is also important to note that we now generally include under the umbrella of the Hundred Years War the Anglo-Scottish wars of the period, which, though concentrated into the period 1296–1357, also rumbled on into the fifteenth century and beyond. It is within these broader contexts, then, that this chapter sets out to assess the effects of the Hundred Years War on the domestic politics and government of England from Edward I to Henry VI.

To do so, it will be convenient to discuss the subject under a number of different heads. We shall begin with the politics of logistics, looking particularly at the ways in which the crown persuaded the political community to provide the manpower and money necessary for the upkeep of its military commitments. We shall then move on to examine the military and diplomatic strategies of the late medieval state in order to see how these were adapted to coincide with the preferred strategies of the polity. Throughout, the emphasis is on the political tension between the foreign ambitions of the crown and the interests of its English subjects, and the degree to which that tension was successfully resolved into the idea of war as a national enterprise.

Manpower and Supplies

To mobilise the community in support of war required the creation of an elaborate administrative infrastructure capable of producing the supplies of manpower, money, shipping, horses, arms and armour, victuals and the whole panoply of services required to keep an army in the field. It was during the period c.1290–c.1360 that the mechanisms for raising and financing armies underwent fundamental changes, and the century that followed was one of refinement rather than reform. Not surprisingly, then, it was also under the three Edwards that some of the fiercest political debates took place over the logistics of war.

The controversies over military service between the 1290s and the 1340s revolved around the distinction between compulsory and voluntary service.[5] Those who held in knight service from the king could be required as part of their feudal obligations to supply fixed quotas of cavalry for service within the king's dominions, free of charge, for a period of forty days: only after that period, or in the event of service in enemy territory, would they normally expect to be paid. Infantry forces could be conscripted by a system known as array, based on the principle that all adult males, free and (after 1285) unfree, had a public duty to assist in the defence of the realm. Edward I, II and III attempted in various ways to increase their rights to both cavalry and infantry service: first, by extending the obligation of the feudal host to fight in 'foreign' theatres of war, such as Flanders in 1297; secondly, by arraying foot soldiers for offensive campaigns in Scotland and requiring that their own communities pay their wages and supply their equipment, as on a number of occasions in the 1310s and 1320s; and, thirdly, by demanding service in person or by substitute on the basis not of feudal tenure but of landed wealth, as in 1297 and again during the mid-1340s. These initiatives provoked widespread opposition: landholders, townsmen and villagers alike protested that they were being taxed twice over, in money and manpower. The crown had little choice but to retreat, and by a series of statutory concessions – notably in 1327 and 1352 – Edward III very largely put an end to these experiments in compulsion.

Such concessions were possible only because the crown was already developing alternative systems of raising volunteer armies. Under this system, known at least from the time of Edward I's crusade and widely adopted for service in France from the 1340s, military commanders and captains contracted with the crown to provide an agreed number of troops at a specified price for a fixed period and undertook to raise those troops themselves through a series of sub-contracts. The crown thus disengaged itself from the process of recruitment and depended instead on the kind of devolved administrative structures noted earlier as a feature of this period. Originally used largely for the provision of cavalry forces for campaigns in which the king himself did not serve, the contract system was extended at least by the 1350s to include the raising of infantry, and became the principal method of recruitment both for offensive campaigns and for the supply of garrison forces for the rest of the Hundred Years War. Its success is also demonstrated by the way it was adapted to provide victuals and arms for such forces: from the middle of the fourteenth century the crown again largely gave up raising such supplies by compulsory purchase and instead contracted with merchants to buy them on the open market.[6]

The impact of this development on the actual conduct of war will be discussed later in this chapter. In assessing the effect that it had on domestic political perceptions, however, it is important to recognise that the emergence of the contract system coincided with, and probably contributed to, important changes in military tactics and strategy which mostly put an end to the mass conscription of relatively poorly trained and equipped foot soldiers and instead favoured small, well disciplined and highly mobile forces made up of men at arms (the traditional heavy cavalry) and mounted archers (that is, longbowmen who fought on foot but moved around on horseback).[7] From the mid-fourteenth century it appears that archers were recruited less from the mass of the peasantry and more from men of yeoman, and even gentle, stock. So far as the cavalry was concerned, the proportions of the nobility and gentry that saw active service in the Scottish and French campaigns of Edward III were probably higher than at almost any other time during the previous two hundred years. Even for these classes, however, the lull in military activity under Richard II and the changes in the objectives and techniques of warfare under Henry V may have reduced participation rates, so that although the titled nobility remained deeply committed to their military vocation, the majority of the gentry withdrew from active campaigning and left the responsibility for the Lancastrian occupation of France to a relatively small number of quasi-professional soldiers. To the extent that political perceptions were coloured by personal experience and that the continuation of the king's wars depended on a sense of unity and purpose built up among the elite, this increasing physical and cultural separation between the domestic polity and the royal armies in the field could be, and has been, seen as the essential explanation of the apparent loss of English interest and commitment during the final phase of the Hundred Years War.[8]

Taxation

The most obvious measure of that loss of commitment is to be found in the amount of money that the English political community was prepared to contribute in taxes to sustain the crown's military efforts both in France and in Scotland. The use of contracts for the recruitment and supplying of royal armies may have been more efficient, but it was also extremely expensive: the idea that all military services had to be purchased put enormous additional pressure on the state and its finances. Between 1294 and 1453 the English exchequer raised in the region of £11,000,000 in direct and indirect taxation (a figure which does not even take into account the victuals, arms and other supplies levied in kind by the crown or the costs borne by individuals and communities in supplying and paying troops before the advent of contracts).[9] Such a statistic only really begins to take on meaning, however, when we realise how it was spread across this 160-year period. Direct taxation, because extraordinary, fluctuated dramatically according to the military and diplomatic situation, with the peaks occurring in the mid-1290s, the years immediately around 1340, the 1370s and the period 1417–22, and with complete or substantial remissions occurring during the years of truce between 1360 and 1369 and in the period 1422–9 when the costs of the war were assumed to have been transferred to Henry VI's new French territories. Indirect taxation, by contrast, raised a good deal less than direct until the 1340s; thereafter, although the king's income from customs and subsidies never reached the same high levels achieved in the 1350s and 1360s, its overall value continued to exceed that from direct taxes for the rest of the Hundred Years War. In discussing the political significance of taxation it is therefore necessary not only to pick up some of the points already addressed in chapters 2 and 4 concerning the record of the parliamentary commons in responding to royal requests for financial assistance but also to ask who actually paid the taxes thus sanctioned and bore the real financial burden of the king's wars.

Whereas service in arms was always a minority activity, direct taxation in later medieval England was, at least in theory, a public obligation bearing alike on laity and clergy, nobleman and commoner, free and unfree. Under the three Edwards the theoretical universality of taxation became more and more a reality and resulted in what appears to have been an increasingly regressive tax regime. In theory at least, taxation of the clergy was reasonably equitable: it was based on income; the poorest were exempt (at least until the 1370s); and the crown was disposed, for reasons of piety, to be reasonably generous with partial or total remissions. The standard basis of assessment for lay taxes, however, was the value of moveable property: chiefly grain and livestock in the countryside and merchandise and household chattels in the towns. Although the gentry and nobility (and, to some extent, the clergy) were liable to such levies, the fact that most moveable wealth lay in the agricultural sector and that most grain and livestock was in the hands of tenant farmers meant that by far the greatest burden of these subsidies was borne by the peasantry. Up to the 1330s, the system provided some protection for the poorest by fixing a minimum valuation for liability; this had the effect of exempting large numbers of smallholders, cottagers and labourers so that in some village communities fewer than a third of householders contributed directly to the king's taxes. In 1334, however, both the taxable minimum and the system of individual assessment were dropped, and each town and vill was instead charged an agreed quota and given the freedom to spread the burden as best suited the local community. Although moveable property generally remained the basis of assessment, this new system allowed the burden of taxation to be spread more widely through the lower strata of society. In particular, it seems that the gentry, who administered the system in conjunction with village elites and urban authorities, sought to offset their own financial problems after the Black Death and to penalise what they saw as an unwarranted improvement in the economic conditions of the peasantry by redistributing the burden of the quotas onto smallholders. This process reached its natural culmination in the poll taxes of 1377, 1379 and 1380 which made taxation a virtually universal obligation binding on all adult heads of population.

The general extension of liability to direct taxation and the particular pressures that the system applied on the lower orders undoubtedly had a powerful part to play in the politicisation of the peasantry: paying taxes was, after all, the most obvious and tangible demonstration of one's obligation to the state. It was also seen, in the generations immediately before and after the Black Death, as a measure of the tyranny that the upper orders were apparently imposing as a result of their control of the political and administrative structures. In the present context, however, it needs to be noted that the trend towards a genuinely comprehensive system of taxation was very largely abandoned after the Peasants' Revolt. The 1334 quotas were re-introduced and there were no further organised efforts to draw the lowest levels of society into the tax net until Tudor times. Indeed, the few fiscal experiments that were attempted during the Lancastrian period were directed not at the labouring classes but at the taxation of the non-beneficed clergy and (more rarely) the exploitation of landed income.

The result was a curious and not altogether satisfactory compromise. On the one hand, those who continued to pay taxes came increasingly to see this as a mark not of subservience but of status: to bear the burden of government was in certain respects to be recognised as part of the polity. It is interesting in this respect to compare the fundamental hostility to Edward III's regressive fiscal policies found in the *Song against the King's Taxes* (*c*.1340) with the much more measured tones of *The Crowned King* (*c*. 1415), in which the existing tax structure, though criticised, was also deemed capable of bearing on 'such as were seemly to suffer the charge'.[10] On the other hand, the increasingly antiquated tax system prevented the crown from exploiting new forms of wealth developing in the century after the Black Death. The comparative generosity of parliaments and convocations in sanctioning taxes, particularly under Edward III and Henry V, disguised this problem for some time. But when public tolerance of taxation declined under Henry VI, the dwindling yield from the lay and clerical subsidies inevitably – even perhaps fatally – compromised the viability of the crown. It therefore appears that while the devolution of administrative responsibility for direct taxes to the localities after 1334 did not in itself adversely affect the finances of the state, the constitutional and practical constraints that prevented the crown from imposing unilateral tax reforms after 1381 did indeed make it increasingly dependent on the fickle support of the political community.

The same tendency towards a static and (from the crown's point of view) increasingly unproductive fiscal system can also be seen in respect of indirect taxation. The customs duties had originally been set up in 1275 to provide a means of paying back the crown's Italian bankers, and until Edward III's reign the income from this source remained relatively modest. Periodically after 1294, however, and permanently after 1342, the revenue from the taxation of overseas trade was greatly boosted by the supplementary subsidies levied on the export of English wool. At first, these subsidies were authorised not by parliament but by groups of merchants, who were persuaded to pay high rates of duty in return for certain trading privileges. It became increasingly obvious, however, that at least part of the real cost of the wool subsidy was being borne by the wool producers and domestic traders in the form of lower prices on the home market. Consequently, the representatives of those interests in the parliamentary commons began from 1340 to claim that they ought to have the exclusive right to authorise this tax. Their ability to persuade the crown of this argument depended largely on their generosity, and from 1342 the wool subsidy became, in effect, a permanent levy successively renewed for fixed periods or, as in 1398, 1415 and 1453, for the term of the king's life. Indirect taxation thus ceased to be extraordinary and became a permanent imposition collected in periods of truce and peace as well as those of active war.

How was the polity reconciled to this development? Since the wool subsidy impacted most obviously on large-scale commercial sheep farming and on the mercantile sector, it bore much more directly than did direct taxation on the active members of the political community. Indeed, it was one of the greatest tributes to Edward III's system of political management that he persuaded these powerful interest groups to undertake such financial liabilities. On the other hand, this experience taught parliament and the polity some powerful lessons for the future. From the later fourteenth century wool exports went into long-term decline, to such an extent that as early as the 1420s, and certainly by the 1440s, they had been outstripped in value by the developing export trade in woollen cloth. Whereas wool exports were taxed at approximately 25–33 per cent of their domestic value, the duties on cloth represented only some 2–6 per cent of the market price.[11] From the crown's point of view, then, the obvious answer was to increase the rates of duty on cloth and, indeed, on other expanding sections of the overseas economy such as the import of luxury goods. But its only success in this respect – the new subsidy of tunnage and poundage instituted under Edward III and Richard II – represented a very modest addition to the fiscal apparatus of the state and in no way compensated for the loss of revenue from wool exports. Whereas the income from the customs and subsidies had represented approximately 18.5 per cent of the total value of overseas trade in the 1350s, it stood at only about 15 per cent in the 1390s and under 12 per cent in the 1440s.[12] The reason for this decline is clear: those economic interests bound up in the production and export of woollen cloth had, through their representatives in parliament, effectively blocked the extension or adaptation of the customs system to match new commercial realities. While the wool growers among the landed elite had an obvious interest in supporting the domestic cloth industry, it is hard to escape the conclusion that in this case the fiscal demands of the state were confounded specifically by the mercantile community acting through the citizens and burgesses in the parliamentary commons. The world of commerce had found a forceful voice in politics and exerted a direct influence on the finances of the crown.

The long Hundred Years War may therefore be said to have witnessed both the triumph and the abasement of the medieval fiscal state. The structures established by Edward I and developed by Edward III allowed the crown, as never before, to exploit the economic resources of the realm. The results, indeed, were alarming: the particularly intense pressures applied in the years 1294–8 and 1337–42 are now generally believed to have had a deeply disruptive impact not only on particular groups of taxpayers but on the whole economy of England.[13] By the same token, however, the development of more powerful political structures allowed the community to resist further extensions of the tax base and to limit the state's fiscal exactions to what were regarded as more tolerable and sustainable levels. The intensely hostile popular reaction to the poll tax of 1380 discredited the idea that the king's demands could simply be passed on to the lower orders and united the polity in an effort to limit the overall burden of royal taxation. It needs to be stressed that this policy did not represent a deliberate conspiracy to impoverish or bankrupt the crown. What it did signify, however, was the equally interesting and increasingly confident assertion that taxation was granted for the benefit of the realm, not merely that of the king. It is in that assertion that we see the beginnings of a genuine notion of public finance.

Justifications for War

To appreciate the criteria by which the political community judged the advantages or liabilities arising from war and thus determined the level of financial commitment, the rest of this chapter will examine the manner in which the crown presented the long Hundred Years War to its English subjects and the degree to which certain groups within society saw their own interests as being advanced by such protracted and expensive commitments. In particular, the following discussion seeks to establish the degree to which the monarchy was able to compensate for the evident failure of coercion, as demonstrated by the contracting out of military recruitment and the devolution of responsibility for raising taxes, by imposing a new political morality which had the effect of engaging its subjects, individually and collectively, in the service of the state.

The obvious starting point for such an analysis lies in the declared war aims of the English crown and its ability to persuade the political community that these were both legitimate and feasible. The basis on which the monarchy fought virtually all wars between the 1290s and the 1450s was, of course, the maintenance of the king's rights. There were, however, notable differences in the way that both the theory and the practice of war were applied in relation to England's two principal enemies. In the case of Scotland, Edward I's initial invasion in 1296 was justified on the basis that John Balliol had rebelled against the suzerainty of the king of England and forfeited his right to rule.[14] The northern realm and its throne were therefore deemed to be in abeyance and under the direct jurisdiction of the English crown. This meant that the ensuing war of conquest could actually be presented as a series of defensive measures and allowed the crown to apply much greater pressure on its subjects for the performance of compulsory military service and the payment of taxes. Under Edward III, however, such arguments had very largely to be dropped. Both the treaty of Edinburgh of 1328 and the setting up of Edward Balliol as king of Scots in 1334 represented an official English acknowledgement that the northern kingdom was a separate (albeit, in the latter case, a dependent) entity and thus a 'foreign' territory; consequently, the argument that the domestic community owed an inescapable obligation of defence was now generally only applied in measures for the protection of the northern shires from continued Scottish raids. Thereafter it was only on very rare occasions – as in Richard II's summons of the feudal host to serve in Scotland in 1385 – that the Scottish wars were presented as a truly national enterprise.[15]

In the case of France, by contrast, the Plantagenets ultimately proved a great deal more successful in binding all their English subjects to the pursuit of their rights. This success is all the more remarkable given the conceptual and practical constraints originally imposed on the monarchy. The duchy of Aquitaine, the focus of the Anglo-French disputes of 1294, 1324 and 1337, was a distant land where the king held a separate title, operated an autonomous regime and presided over an elite that had few close cultural or political associations with England. The thirteenth century had witnessed the development of an idea that the Plantagenet dominions comprised a fixed federation whose parts could not be alienated and which were all in some sense incorporated within the rights of the 'crown'. But although Edward I played upon this notion in his demands for English contributions towards the Gascon war of 1294–8, it is noticeable that he and his successors also found it necessary in their domestic propaganda to stress the direct threat posed to the security of *England* by a hostile French monarchy with designs to attack the realm and (as Edward I and III both expressed it) to wipe the English tongue from the face of the earth.[16] Furthermore, when the Anglo-French disputes extended outside those territories in south-western France to which the Plantagenets had a proper claim, it became even more important that the crown should develop adequate arguments to justify the resulting requests for English military service in genuinely 'foreign' lands.[17] Edward I found no proper answer to this problem when he attempted to intervene in Flanders in 1297.[18] But Edward III's decision formally to style himself king of France in 1340 had the effect of imposing on the English political community a direct moral and legal obligation to support his general policy of intervention both in Flanders and in other provinces of the French crown. Throughout the following two decades the parliamentary rhetoric and propaganda of Edward's domestic regime consistently presented the war in France as an enterprise intended both to recover the king's rights (which, significantly, were not defined) and to guarantee the integrity of the realm of England. By such means was the principle of urgent necessity, originally developed primarily in reference to defensive measures, now successfully extended to commit the entire nation to the pursuit of an offensive foreign war.[19]

Such policies also carried risks. It was all too easy for the political community to become convinced of the legitimacy and viability of the crown's more ambitious strategies and therefore to become disillusioned when confronted with peace proposals that appeared to compromise the king's rights and the nation's interests. One obvious instance of this phenomenon was the failure of Edward III and his successors to avenge the shameful peace of 1328 by reviving Edward I's claims to direct sovereignty – or even, after 1357, to feudal suzerainty – over Scotland: the apparent fulfilment of the ideal of Scottish independence articulated in the Declaration of Arbroath was a regular cause of embarrassment to historically-minded Englishmen in the late fourteenth and fifteenth centuries.[20] From the time of the treaty of Brétigny there was also a potential and sometimes dangerous conflict between the heightened expectations of a population fed on Edward III's imperialistic propaganda and the uncomfortable realities of Anglo-French diplomacy.[21] When in 1394 Richard II presented to parliament a peace proposal requiring him to revert to the practice used before 1337 and perform homage for the duchy of Aquitaine, for example, the knights of the shire simply refused to countenance the move, complaining that 'every single Englishman having the king of England as his lord would pass under the heel of the French king and be kept for the future under the yoke of slavery'.[22] Arguably still more serious was the flaw in Henry V's particular justification for the new phase of the French war that began in 1415. In his domestic propaganda Henry concentrated not on the protection of the realm or the conquest of its ancient enemy but on the recovery of his own legitimate titles and inheritances in France. This renewed emphasis on the pursuit of the king's personal rights meant that the making and fulfilment of the treaty of Troyes were regarded as the natural end to England's military commitment: thereafter, it was Henry VI's French subjects who could bear the cost of establishing Plantagenet rule across the Channel.[23] The domestic regime was therefore faced with a deeply embarrassing situation as it was forced to admit that this process had failed and that the continuing war effort would have to be funded from England. Unfortunately for Henry VI's advisors, any attempts they made to revert to Edward III's propaganda techniques and revive national commitment to a public cause were effectively confounded by the news of the Valois advance and the increasing sense of personal and political separation between the English of England and the English in France.

In many ways, then, the justifications for war presented by successive kings to their English subjects only proved credible so long as the rhetoric of propaganda was seen to be consistent with the realities of diplomacy. Further than this, indeed, it became increasingly obvious, as the fourteenth and fifteenth centuries progressed, that strategies devised purely for the pursuit of the king's rights had necessarily to be reconciled with, and in some cases adapted to, the interests of certain powerful lobbies within the domestic political community. The process by which the king's war aims evolved to incorporate these interests can be demonstrated with specific reference to the two groups that arguably did most to make long-term and large-scale war a viable proposition: namely, the landed elite and the merchants.

War and the Aristocracy

It is often remarked that medieval (and indeed later) aristocracies regarded war as a natural state, in the sense that it allowed them the opportunity to justify their privileged status by fulfilling their function as fighters. It is equally clear, however, that some wars were a great deal more popular with the medieval English aristocracy than others. The remarkable re-militarisation of the landed elite – both nobility and gentry – during the fourteenth century must be accounted for not so much by the revival of older traditions of service during the Scottish campaigns of Edward I and Edward III but by the altogether more glamorous and more lucrative careers of those who fought with the latter king and his lieutenants on the fields of France. That is not to say, of course, that the Scottish wars did not have a formative effect on the northern aristocracy: indeed, it was the need to provide a regular system for patrolling the march and maintaining order in the north that accounted in large part for the elevation of certain baronial families – particularly the Percys and the Nevilles – into the ranks of the titled nobility during the later fourteenth century.[24] In general, however, it was to France that most of the elite instinctively looked after Edward III's time as the best source of those two most important advantages of war: honour and profit.

Many historians have assumed that there was some kind of innate conflict between the search for honour and the desire for material gain during the Hundred Years War, contrasting the fantasy world of chivalry with the harsh realities of the mercenary instinct. In the present context, it is perhaps sufficient to notice that profit had more often than not to be measured in non-material ways. It is now fashionable to play down the more spectacular examples of the ransoms, booty and other accidents of war enjoyed by English men at arms such as Sir Thomas Holand in the fourteenth century or Sir John Fastolf in the fifteenth and to emphasise the more typical case of John Talbot, whose gains of war actually only just allowed him to cover his considerable costs.[25] It is true that many individual men at arms could enjoy a good war even when the general strategic position looked bleak, and that the *perception* of war as a profit-making exercise remained remarkably enduring.[26] Nevertheless, to see the contract system as turning war from a vocation into a business is to mistake the motivations of the landed elite and to forget the extraordinary degree of tolerance normally demonstrated by military contractors at the frequent failure of the crown to pay up: neither the Percy rebellion of 1403 nor Richard of York's opposition to the Lancastrian regime in the 1450s, for example, can be explained simply in terms of the undoubtedly substantial military debts owed to them by the king's exchequer.[27] Thus, while the polity at large, through its representatives in parliament, gave increasing emphasis during the fifteenth century to financial rectitude as an element within the 'good governance' required of the monarchy, there is little to suggest that the ability or inability of the crown to balance the war account explained the withdrawal of aristocratic support at the end of the Hundred Years War.

Ultimately, therefore, the factor that did most to dictate the degree of aristocratic participation in war was indeed the pursuit of honour. The countless tomb effigies, brasses, stained glass windows, armorial bearings and private chapels erected in English churches to commemorate members of the military elite in the course of the Hundred Years War provide perhaps the most striking evidence now at our disposal of the prestige that accrued both to established and to parvenu families from their active involvement in the crown's great enterprises. In many respects, then, this is precisely the area in which the interests of the individual and those of the crown most clearly and easily overlapped. In particular, the state sponsorship of the cult of chivalry that is such a feature of political strategy from Edward I's time and which reached its perfect manifestation in Edward III's Order of the Garter provides important evidence of the way in which the essential individualism of knightly culture could be institutionalised and mobilised in the service of the state. Honour itself could be a collective – even a 'political' – experience.

On the other hand, it is also clear that war remained an essentially freelance profession in the later Middle Ages and that the crown was often unable, for practical as well as political reasons, to guarantee the obedience of its noble and knightly supporters to the official command structures. Edward III, for example, found it particularly embarrassing when the English forces operating in northern France simply ignored both the truce of Bordeaux of 1357 and the treaty of Brétigny and continued what was essentially a private – and, for them, a highly productive – war. Although the military reforms of Henry V and the particular disciplines imposed on the permanent garrisons in Normandy in the fifteenth century did much to reduce this problem, it is arguable that no king of this period ever really overcame the more substantial problem of having to divert or compromise his own grand strategy in order to appease his commanders and cavalry officers. The *chevauchées* of Edward III, the Black Prince and John of Gaunt proved very popular with all ranks, who were able to lord it over the non-combatant population of France and return to England laden with booty; but some historians at least would argue that these great marches had little strategic value and diverted attention away from the more immediate task of recovering control in Aquitaine and organising a more systematic occupation of northern France. In particular, the continuing desire of members of the high nobility to establish their political credibility at home by undertaking high-profile continental campaigns sometimes meant that valuable resources were squandered in fruitless and sometimes disastrous adventures: the expeditions of Thomas of Woodstock in 1380 and of John Beaufort in 1443 provide two very obvious examples of this phenomenon.[28]

All of this is not to suggest that the military command of the Hundred Years War represented some kind of organised chaos: it is clear that Edward III and Henry V provided just the brand of charismatic and forceful leadership that ensured a high degree of cohesion within the upper ranks of their armies. What it does suggest is that the pursuit of the crown's rights depended on, and at times perhaps was compromised to, the war aims of the aristocracy. When the work of Joan of Arc and Charles VII threw the Plantagenets' own rights into jeopardy, the link between the honour of the crown and the honour of England was inevitably revived in certain quarters: witness Sir John Fastolf's impassioned arguments against the peace terms put forward at the Congress of Arras in 1435 or Richard of York's comments in the Shrewsbury manifesto of 1452 on the 'derogation, lesion of honour and villainy reported generally unto the English nation' by the collapse of the Lancastrian regime in France.[29] But these, of course, were *ex parte* statements from active participants in the last stages of the war. The majority particularly of the lesser aristocracy, as we have noted, had long since withdrawn from the continental struggle and presumably found it at least slightly easier to stomach the loss of national honour by knowing that they were not personally implicated in it. Once again, we return to the point that the loss of France rested perhaps above all in the failure of Henry VI's government to reconcile royal policy with the will of the polity.

War and the Merchants

The other group in English political society that was crucial to the successful maintenance of war and whose interests had therefore to be accommodated within the strategy of the crown were the merchants.[30] The collapse of the Italian banking companies during the 1340s and the simultaneous switch to a heavy dependence on indirect taxation made the crown doubly indebted to the English merchants, who not only paid the customs duties but now also acted as some of the principal suppliers of ready cash in the form of government loans. Until the early 1350s, Edward III relied on small groups of English merchant capitalists who were granted monopolies or privileges in the export trade as both inducement and recompense for their large investments in the state. It became increasingly apparent, however, that these syndicates were jeopardising the interests both of the wool growers and of the majority of those merchants who dealt in wool on the domestic market. The capture of the major continental port of Calais in 1347 offered an unexpected opportunity to resolve these conflicts. In the process, it is possible to see how royal policy shifted subtly but decisively away from its own purely strategic concerns and towards the preservation of English commercial interests.

Calais offered a very convenient base through which English armies might enter and leave France, and it was promptly invested with a garrison that quickly became, and remained, the single largest military force in the permanent pay of the English crown. By 1421, it was calculated that Calais cost the equivalent of a third of the regular revenues of the English state (that is, including indirect taxation but excluding direct subsidies).[31] It is not surprising, then, that this financial commitment should have figured large among the on-going costs of defence cited regularly by the crown in its requests for parliamentary taxation from the 1360s onwards. But king and council were also well aware that such appeals were likely to prove popular among the groups represented in parliament. By the fifteenth century the Calais garrison had become a kind of military academy for the English landed classes; as a result, its members could bring a quite extraordinary pressure to bear on both parliament and the crown to ensure that their interests – and, in particular, the payment of their wages – were given high priority.[32] More specifically in the present context, Calais also offered very considerable commercial benefits. The establishment of the staple (the compulsory entrepôt through which all English wool had to pass on its way to continental markets) at Calais in 1363 was organised in such a way as to protect the interests both of the merchant capitalists and of the domestic wool producers and lesser wool traders. The preservation and guarantee of this staple therefore became central to the political agenda of the commons during the later fourteenth century and gave added force to the public argument that Calais was perhaps the most vital of all English possessions on the continent.

What is perhaps most interesting is that these arguments continued to be articulated long after Calais turned from an asset into an economic liability. The English Company of the Staple at Calais, originally formed simply to administer the town, began in the later fourteenth century to take on some of the attributes of the earlier mercantile syndicates, winning certain exclusive privileges in return for the large sums of money that its members were prepared to lend to the crown. In 1429–30, in a misguided attempt to encourage the flow of precious metals into English mints, the government of Henry VI implemented the Bullion and Partition Ordinances, which forbade the use of credit transactions in the staple and insisted that all wool bought by foreign merchants at Calais be paid for in silver and gold. The ordinances could not have been implemented without the collaboration of the staplers, or, to put it more precisely, a group of leading members of the company, who sought in return still greater control of England's export trade in wool. But the experiment had disastrous consequences: the wool markets collapsed and the duke of Burgundy, whose merchants were among the chief victims, withdrew from the English alliance in 1435 and mounted a full-scale siege of Calais. The wool trade itself never fully recovered. And yet both the staple and the monopoly company remained in force. By this stage the only real justification for the company lay in its ability to provide loans to the crown and assist in the financing of the garrison; the final irony in this complex story rests in the fact that the restrictive practices promoted by the staplers inevitably reduced the profits of indirect taxation that were so often used as security in their credit transactions and thus left the crown without the means to repay them. It is difficult, then, to resist the conclusion that a war fought in the defence of the nation's wealth became not only a liability to its overall prosperity but also a means of preserving the economic interests and political influence of an increasingly small but powerful section of the merchant class.

This, however, is not necessarily the way in which contemporaries viewed the situation. One reason why the siting of the staple at Calais had originally been acceptable to wool growers and lesser merchants was that it prevented foreigners from entering England to buy wool directly, thus putting a bigger share of the market in the hands of denizens and producing economic benefits for the country as a whole. The wool staple therefore became a source of inspiration to those groups that sought, with some success, to apply a range of punitive measures against the alien merchants who continued to trade in wool and, more importantly, in other unregulated commodities (including cloth) during the first half of the fifteenth century. The combination of strategic and economic advantages supposedly offered by Calais, coupled with periodic scares over its continued security, created powerful opposition to any government that demonstrated less than total commitment to the preservation of the town: both the anonymous poem *The Libelle of Englyshe Polycye* (1436) and the debates in the parliament of 1437 demonstrated an abiding conviction that Calais was the essential key to England's commercial prosperity as well as to her military security.[33] Because both the garrison and the staple of Calais survived the final withdrawal of the English forces from the rest of France around 1450, the domestic political did not therefore have to confront the economic consequences of defeat in quite the same way that it was forced to explain away the loss of honour. But to the historian at least there can be no doubt that the argument that the Hundred Years War was fought for the preservation of England's material interests had become increasingly less general and more and more sectional in its real application as the fifteenth century progressed. As with the aristocracy, so with the merchants: war, which had once been a joint stock enterprise, had become simply a means of preserving vested minority interests.

Popular Responses to War

Whereas the nobility, gentry and merchants enjoyed the political influence necessary to have a direct impact on military and diplomatic policy, the only way in which the commonalty could really affect the making of war was by the degree of compliance it demonstrated to the king's demands for contributions. While popular approaches to war were therefore usually only reactive, they have as valid and important a place in the study of late medieval political life as do the attitudes of the elite, not least because, under extreme circumstances, they could actually provide a major distraction from the business of fighting. It is hardly possible here to discuss all aspects of the public response to the Hundred Years War, so by way of conclusion to this chapter we shall concentrate particularly on the degree of popular resistance demonstrated to the activities of the war state during the fourteenth and first half of the fifteenth centuries.

It now seems likely that the most intense pressures applied by the crown during the period covered by this book arose during the opening stages of Edward III's French war in 1337–42, when the country had to sustain not only a continuous series of standard lay and clerical taxes but also a number of still more onerous experimental taxes in wool and other agricultural produce. These levies, coupled with the conscription of soldiers and the appropriation of foodstuffs to supply royal armies, led to widespread discontent and produced rumours in both official sources and popular literature that the country was ripe for revolt.[34] That no such revolt actually occurred can be explained in a number of ways: the absence both of a popular demagogue and of a single political figure who might be used as a scapegoat for the king's mistakes is one possibility; the tendency to bemoan the corruption that accompanied the collection of taxes rather than to question the validity of the levies themselves provides another. Perhaps most interesting in the present context, however, is the suggestion that organised resistance before the Black Death was much more likely to be directed against seigneurial than royal demands, a point that inevitably raises further important, and still largely unanswered, questions about the relative burden of feudal and state exactions both in this period and indeed in the generations following the plague.[35]

By 1381, however, much had undoubtedly changed. The years of English military success in the 1340s and 1350s had encouraged those less well informed of the realities of strategy that Edward III's claim to the throne of France might indeed be fulfilled. The military reversals suffered after 1369 created widespread suspicion that the vast amounts of money collected for the war were being wasted in unproductive campaigns and mismanaged by the unscrupulous advisors surrounding the boy-king Richard II. In particular, John of Gaunt now emerged as the focus of much popular political frustration. Furthermore, the communities of the coastal shires in south-east England were increasingly concerned about the possibility, and the occasional reality, of French raids and the apparent failure of the government to provide adequate means of defence.[36] What finally provoked the Peasants' Revolt, of course, was the controversy surrounding the administration of the third poll tax. Not since 1332 had the central government involved itself in the registration and assessment of individual taxpayers; consequently, when the crown refused to accept the returns made by the collectors of the poll tax and sent judicial commissions into certain shires to inquire into the way in which the levy had been administered, it was seen to be challenging a long-standing system that protected both the privacy of the taxpayer and the autonomy of the peasant leaders and minor gentry who acted as local tax gatherers.[37] Although there was inevitably no shortage of hostility to seigneurial authority in the ensuing rebellion, it is possible to argue that the Peasants' Revolt was much more an attack on, and a crisis of, the state than of feudal lordship; in which case, it can also undoubtedly be taken as the supreme example of the politicisation of the peasantry in later medieval England.

After 1381, there was no further significant popular reaction to the war until the time of Henry VI. The manifestos put out by Archbishop Scrope of York during his rebellion against Henry IV in 1405 certainly employed the usual motifs of heavy taxation and inadequate defence as a means of exciting popular support, but the real aim of the revolt was to challenge Henry IV's right to the throne.[38] The tolerance demonstrated towards the next concentrated military and fiscal effort – that of Henry V – has largely to be explained in terms of that king's extraordinary ability to motivate and mobilise the realm in his service. But just as the heightening of popular expectations under Edward III had increased the general sense of disillusionment during the minority of Richard II, so did the achievements – and the considerable propaganda campaign – of Henry V almost inevitably rebound on the regime of his son.

It has been implied above that there may well have been a degree of disengagement, even indifference, on the part of some members of the active polity to the events of 1449–50 when English forces were finally induced to withdraw from Normandy. By contrast, there was little sense of inevitability or relief in the violent popular disturbances that ensued. Some of those who took matters into their own hands in 1450 were themselves members of the military: Adam Moleyns, the former keeper of the privy seal, was murdered at Portsmouth by a band of mutinous soldiers, while the disgraced duke of Suffolk was put to death by a group of sailors claiming, interestingly enough, to be acting on behalf of the 'community of the realm'.[39] But the scale and vehemence of the popular reaction cannot be accounted for solely by the demobilisation of aggrieved troops. Those who participated in the principal rising, led by Jack Cade, were drawn from a wide range of the non-combatant population of Kent, including gentlemen and peasants, craftsmen and tradesmen; in particular, the presence of large numbers of those involved in the manufacture of cloth, who were suffering directly as a result of the recent disruption of trade with Flanders, provides a particularly striking example of the way in which the war had impinged not only on the consciousnesses but on the actual livelihoods of the king's ordinary subjects.

In certain respects, however, the strong sense of frustration demonstrated by the rebels of 1450 could indeed be said to have chimed with the prevailing attitude of the political elite. It was generally agreed that the war had been lost because of poor management at Westminster and poor leadership in the field; the possibility that it had foundered for lack of political will and financial commitment on the part of the English community was either conveniently ignored or genuinely discounted. This chapter has cautioned against the idea that the entire population, or even those actively involved in politics at the central and local levels, were ever completely united in support of the military policies of the crown; the image of the Hundred Years War as the first great national enterprise in our island history was a convenient fiction created by contemporary chroniclers, Tudor playwrights, and modern film makers to celebrate the achievements of Edward III and Henry V. From the popular perspective, indeed, the greatest irony of the Hundred Years War lies in the fact that defeat always tended to prove a more energising force than did victory: the experiences that did most to unite the community were those involving the loss of the king's rights and the consequent disgrace of the realm. In this sense at least, the Hundred Years War provided the one experience capable of uniting the great mass of the population of later medieval England into a self-consciously political society.

6

POLITICAL ISSUES: JUSTICE

Recent scholarship has come more and more to appreciate that justice lay at the very heart of political life in the later Middle Ages. Because so much attention has been given to the study of crime in medieval society, we are perhaps too inclined to think of the politics of justice simply in terms of a debate on public order. In fact, the notion of justice encompassed – as it still encompasses – a much wider range of issues concerning the stability of society, the preservation of public morality, and the sanctity of property: in other words, the principles by which governance was justified and legitimately implemented. The late medieval debate on justice was therefore a discourse upon the very way in which the polity regulated itself and ran the kingdom.[1]

The Scope and Structure of Royal Justice

Pre-dating the fiscal developments discussed in the previous chapter, and of still greater importance in its long-term impact on politics, was a series of judicial reforms – a veritable legal revolution – instituted by the governments of Henry III and Edward I. The effect of these changes was vastly to increase the scope and scale of royal justice. Whereas prior to the mid-thirteenth century the tribunals that operated at, or from, the centre (most notably the court of common pleas, the general eyre and the assize circuits) had been restricted in the main to the hearing of pleas of debt and property disputes and the trial of serious crimes punishable by death (treasons and felonies), after *c.*1250 they also admitted a mass of private litigation concerning petty crimes punishable merely by fine (the class of offences known as trespasses). At first, the crown would accept trespass actions only if the cases alleged had been committed 'with force and arms' (*vi et armis*), a restriction that incidentally requires us to adopt a critical approach to the often very formulaic descriptions of acts of violence found in much late medieval trespass litigation. By the end of the fourteenth century, however, the concept of trespass had also been extended to cover a whole range of non-violent crimes such as bribery, the use of false weights and measures and notably, after the Ordinance and Statute of Labourers, the taking of excessive wages. The implications of all these developments were obvious and the results already apparent by the end of the thirteenth century: namely, a major increase in the competence, and therefore also in the business, of the king's courts.[2]

This legal revolution, like the one earlier effected by Henry II, is to be explained not simply in terms of a thrusting monarchy and an ambitious central government but also as a product of increased demand from below. It is particularly interesting to notice that the new action of trespass was seized upon by peasants as an effective means of resolving their disputes: the business of the courts increased not simply because the landed classes became more litigious but also because the range of remedies offered by the crown had become applicable and available to a much larger number of people.[3] Pressures of this kind not infrequently exceed what can realistically be delivered, and a good deal of the grumbling that went on about the supposed failure of royal justice in the fourteenth and fifteenth centuries can be explained in terms of the new and perhaps unrealistically high hopes of a larger political community brought into much closer contact with the king's laws and the king's judges. The disingenuousness of much of this debate is demonstrated by the fact that political society, far from rejecting the new judicial procedures developed by the government of

Henry III and Edward I, brought added pressure to bear on their successors to extend the crown's judicial competence still further. Two particular examples from the period immediately after the Black Death have recently been explored: the new actions linked to the law of contracts; and the development of trespass on the case, which facilitated the punishment of those who had failed to fulfil occupational and ethical obligations.[4] Equally significant was the emergence, in the same period, of the royal chancery as a court of equity, dispensing an institutionalised form of the royal grace in order to resolve the increasing number of disputes for which the common law provided no answer. Although there is no comprehensive and accurate measure of the total amount of business done in the various royal courts during the later Middle Ages, the dramatic growth of the common plea rolls, which more than doubled in size over the period covered by this book, gives at least some clue to the extraordinary explosion of private litigation experienced in the king's courts.[5] It also provides powerful, if circumstantial, evidence in favour of the thesis that during the later Middle Ages litigation increasingly replaced violence as the first (if by no means always the last) resort in dispute settlement.[6]

The other major consequence of the legal revolution was the development of a new judicial structure. By the end of the thirteenth century the expansion in crown business was putting a great strain on the existing courts and their personnel. Down to Edward I's time, the centrepiece of royal justice was the general eyre, an itinerant commission staffed by the judges and serjeants of the central courts, sent out into the shires to hear assizes, investigate the crown's feudal and fiscal rights and deal with felonies. When the eyre began to take cognisance of trespasses, however, its workload increased dramatically, thus slowing down proceedings and making it increasingly difficult for the court to fulfil what was regarded as its basic responsibility to visit each shire at least once every seven years. The last national visitation of the eyre was called off in 1294.[7] It is important to acknowledge that this postponement was occasioned not by the administrative collapse of the institution but by the need to exempt landowners from the threat of impending litigation and thus free them to participate in Edward I's war for the defence of Gascony. Indeed, the eyre was to be revived in

1329 and might have been re-established as a regular part of the judicial framework had not Edward III abruptly ended the experiment on seizing power from Mortimer and Isabella in the following year. Nevertheless, the visitation of 1329–30 also re-awakened the political controversy that had attached itself to the eyre in the thirteenth century. The general eyre was intended as much for the protection of royal rights as for the provision of justice and had long been viewed as an unwelcome intrusion, a breach of the tradition that royal government in the shires should be carried out by, and in the interests of, the local power elites. Any attempt to restore the eyre, either in name or in substance, during the fourteenth century was therefore almost bound to be resisted by the county communities through their newly vocal representatives in the parliamentary commons.[8]

The obvious question therefore arose as to how the judicial system ought to be adapted to meet the pressures that politics, as well as the increase particularly in criminal actions, had placed upon it. For some time, the crown prevaricated. Throughout the first half of the fourteenth century it experimented variously with provincial sessions of the central court of king's bench, with extraordinary criminal tribunals nicknamed trailbastons (from the bastons or sticks carried by criminal bands), and with local commissions of 'oyer and terminer' empowered to 'hear and determine' indictments. By the middle of the fourteenth century, however, the monarchy had come to accept that it needed to provide standing commissions in each shire capable of receiving indictments and delivering judgment in cases both of trespass and of felony. The result was the emergence of the justices of the peace.

The English local magistracy originally grew from the policing and military functions of an older group of local officials known as the keepers of the peace.[9] On a number of occasions after 1329, the keepers were temporarily empowered not only to receive indictments but also to judge offences brought before them by juries of presentment and private bills of trespass. What really transformed the keepers of the peace into justices of the peace, however, was the economic dislocation created by the Black Death and the great logistical challenge of enforcing the Statute of Labourers. The creation of standing commissions in the shires, staffed mainly by local gentry and empowered to deliver judgment and impose sentence upon those who contravened the new labour legislation, had a major impact on the way that both the central government and the county communities perceived their respective responsibilities to preserve the king's peace. After 1361, with only two brief intermissions, groups of magnates, gentry and local men of law, assisted by judges and serjeants of the central courts, were given permanent responsibility to enforce the criminal law within the shires.[10] Although most cases involving men of rank and influence would subsequently be transferred into the superior criminal court of king's bench, the quarter sessions of the justices of the peace thus became the courts of first instance for a significant proportion of all felony and trespass prosecutions brought in late medieval England.

For several generations, historians have presented the rise of the justices of the peace in terms of a power struggle between the centre and the localities, a struggle that ended in defeat for the crown and victory for the polity. It has therefore become the classic example of the fourteenth-century transformation from law state to war state discussed in the introduction to chapter 5. Because the peace commissions were supposedly dominated by the county gentry, they are assumed to have symbolised – and guaranteed – the general determination of the shire communities to preserve their autonomy and ensure that landed society, rather than the monarchy, remained the most immediate source of authority in the localities. So successful were the representatives of the shires in using their new-found control over taxation to bargain with the king for the devolution of criminal justice that the resulting judicial structure not only outlived the Hundred Years War and the supposed return to central control under the Tudors but continued to provide an essential check on the expansion of the bureaucratic state until as late as the nineteenth century. More particularly from the present point of view, the decentralisation of justice supposedly alienated power from the state and vested it in the hands of local elites who used it not to promote the king's peace but to advance their own interests. According to this viewpoint, the war state did not merely replace the law state in the priorities of the crown; it virtually destroyed it.[11]

Such an over-arching thesis almost inevitably invites criticism, and recent scholarship has begun to question some of the supposed political implications of the changes wrought to the judicial structure during the fourteenth century. Three qualifications are of particular importance. First, it has been pointed out that the parliamentary commons cannot in fact be proved to have developed a coherent programme in favour of judicial devolution until at least the 1340s, and were much more inclined to respond to government action than to initiate change themselves.[12] Secondly, it has been demonstrated that the supposed distinction between centre and locality was already blurred as a result of the collaboration during the early fourteenth century between the king's judges and the local gentry and men of law in the assize and gaol delivery sessions.[13] Thirdly, it has been shown that the regular appointment of justices and serjeants from the central courts to the commissions of the peace from the 1340s onwards helped not only to guarantee a professional presence on the bench for at least half a century but also permanently to integrate the quarter sessions into the wider judicial structure of which they were merely a part.[14] The last point in particular helps us also to understand the cultural, as well as the purely structural, significance of the commissions of the peace. The English magistracy came into being at precisely the time that the traditional seigneurial authority enjoyed by the landed elite was coming under attack; by seeking to bolster their position through the exercise of public authority delegated to them by the crown, the upper orders were not so much usurping the functions of central government as extending and employing them in the pursuit of social, economic and political stability. Indeed, it has recently been argued that the very identity of the English 'gentry' rests in the process by which the knightly classes were transformed into agents of the state.[15]

To appreciate the true significance of the changes taking place in the judicial structure in the fourteenth century, then, we have to move away from the slightly artificial distinction between centre and locality and see the rise of the justices of the peace as part of a more general increase in the capacity of English governance. On the other hand, this begs the question as to the purpose and the nature of the government thus dispensed. By giving the elite an important role to play in the operation of royal justice, did the crown simply make it easier for the more powerful members of local society to subvert the judicial structure and use it for the pursuit of their own political and social primacy? And if the quantity of justice provided by the crown undoubtedly increased during the later Middle Ages, what of its quality? To answer such questions we shall proceed from the bottom up, beginning with the responses of the peasantry and then progressing, via a discussion of the use and abuse of the law by the gentry and nobility, to a final appreciation of the new responsibilities and pressures that the system of justice imposed on the monarchy.

Attitudes to Justice: the Peasantry

The preceding chapters have suggested that the demographic, economic and social changes brought on by the plague resulted, by the fifteenth century, in a larger and more diverse polity. However, as the earlier discussion of regressive taxation shows, this does not preclude the possibility that in the mid-fourteenth century the apparatus of the state was indeed taken over by the proprietary classes in an effort to maintain their own interests. Justice was an obvious weapon in the campaign launched after the Black Death to perpetuate a closed elite. The labour legislation of 1349–51 and the judicial structure created for its enforcement had a particularly startling effect on the relationship between lords and labourers by shifting much of the litigation on wages and contracts from the private jurisdiction of the manor to the public forum of the king's courts. Although the justices of the peace were ultimately unable to counteract the upward movement of wages, there is much evidence to indicate that the new tribunals created in the shires offered landholders and other employers an unparalleled opportunity to proceed in a particularly brutal fashion against employees whose lesser social standing almost inevitably destined them to condemnation.[16]

Nor were wage labourers the only victims of the reaction now launched by landed society in alliance with the state. Feudal lords also sought the assistance of the crown and the common law in their campaign to re-establish rights over their villein tenants.[17] Most significantly of all, the rise of the peace commissions had the effect of challenging (potentially, if not always in reality) the right of each village community to undertake its own system of crime prevention and control through self-policing mechanisms such as the office of constable, the surety group, the watch, and the hue and cry. It has been convincingly argued that Wat Tyler's demand in 1381 that there be no law but 'the law of Winchester' was a reference not, as previously thought, to Domesday Book, but to the statute of Winchester of 1285, in which many of these older obligations for the maintenance of public order were enshrined.[18] Thus, the generation between the Black Death and the Peasants' Revolt can indeed be seen as one of symbolic, and sometimes actual, political exclusion, during which the landed classes operated an increasingly coercive system of governance designed to preserve an older and already antiquated vision of the social and political order.

Under such circumstances, it is also easy to understand why the royal courts and their agents should have been singled out for such intense criticism in popular literature and political action during the fourteenth century. The idea that the courts operated on the basis of money and influence rather than of reason was obviously not new, but became a particular preoccupation in this period. The Latin tag *si dedero* (literally 'if I shall give', that is, give a bribe) appears in texts as diverse as John Ball's seditious letters and John Gower's *Vox clamantis* and seems to have been used as a kind of shorthand representation of corruption in popular criticism of the courts: as a political poem of the early fourteenth century puts it, 'No man may come truth to, but he sing *si didero*.'[19] Such prevailing attitudes also help to explain the particularly violent reaction against representatives of the judicial and legal system during the Peasants' Revolt. The decapitation, at Lakenheath in Suffolk, of Sir John Cavendish, the chief justice of the court of king's bench, and the macabre puppet show made at Bury St Edmunds with his head and that of the prior of the monastery, were merely the most striking of a whole series of violent episodes directed against members of the judicial hierarchy. More particularly, however, the attacks on justices of the peace and the active participation of significant numbers of village elders in the revolt of 1381 can probably best be explained by the way in which the peace commissions were seen to have impinged on the responsibilities previously undertaken by leading peasants in local peace-keeping.[20] There can be little doubt that in 1381 a very substantial and perhaps increasing proportion of the English population regarded itself as effectively excluded from the king's justice.

How much did this situation change after the Peasants' Revolt? In the immediate aftermath of the rising, it was necessary for the preservation of stability that the state respond in some positive if token way to popular criticisms of the legal system. The government's answer was to temper the harshness of the reaction threatened in the quarter sessions by withdrawing the powers of the existing justices of the peace and limiting the new commissioners appointed in 1382 to the receiving of indictments: the power to render judgments was now handed over to special oyer and terminer commissions directed by royal lawyers drawn from the central courts. In 1389, however, the determining powers of the justices of the peace were finally restored, and over the next few years the quorum (the smaller group of named commissioners who had to be present for judgment and sentencing) was extended to include not only the assize justices but also local men of law.[21] In the end, then, the revolt of 1381, far from discrediting the peace commissions, simply reinforced their place in the judicial hierarchy and resulted in a further shift of responsibility from centre to locality. The quarter sessions thus continued to provide the ideal forum in which the powerful and wealthy could use their influence over the system of criminal justice to control the peasantry: in particular, the threat of the labour laws presumably long continued an irksome irritation to those workers seeking wages that reflected the real state of the market rather than the official rates fixed by the courts.[22]

Much the same sense of helplessness must also have been experienced in civil litigation brought in the central courts when the rival parties were drawn from different ranks in society. In Cade's Rebellion of 1450, for example, it was claimed that the 'poor people and commons of the realm' were losing their titles to land and their ability to prove them through law as a result of the machinations of the 'gentle' and (significantly for this period) the members of the royal household.[23] And even without such interference, the straightforward cost of litigation itself was often prohibitive: the poor Kentishman who took himself off to London to obtain redress in the royal courts in the anonymous fifteenth-century poem *London Lickpenny* found himself repeatedly thwarted for lack of financial resources and retired home, vowing to meddle no more in the law.[24] The common complaint that only the rich can afford the luxury of justice obviously neither began, nor ended, in the later Middle Ages.

Alongside such abiding prejudices, however, there is also a certain amount of evidence to suggest that the fifteenth century witnessed a new realism on the part not only of the law-enforcers but also of at least the more substantial peasants who found it possible to work with, and even benefit from, the structure of royal justice (the parallels with the gradual accommodation of the crown's fiscal demands in the same period is obvious). The justices of the peace did not, in the end, infringe upon the rights of village elites to maintain local policing: indeed, it became clear that the quarter sessions could only operate effectively with the active co-operation of the constables of vills and the bailiffs of hundreds.[25] In 1388–90 the justices of the peace were permitted to set reasonable wage rates at their own discretion; although the poor survival of fifteenth-century peace rolls makes it difficult to assess whether this really resulted in a more flexible and lenient approach to the enforcement of the labour laws, it should be remembered that the new class of agricultural employers, the yeomen, lacked the coercive authority of the nobility and gentry and were much less inclined to ferment animosity among villagers by prosecuting them in the quarter sessions.[26] It is interesting, then, that when the commons of Kent articulated their grievances against the justices of the peace in 1450, they actually complained not about the tyranny of the criminal law or the quality of justice dispensed by the bench but about the practical inconveniences caused by having to travel long distances to get to court.[27] Finally, the continued expansion of routine litigation in the court of common pleas on minor civil disputes – above all, pleas of debt – stands as striking testimony to the long-term shift of judicial activity away from both the manor and the hundred and county courts and to the capacity of the crown to provide a wide range of practical remedies at least for the upper ranks of the free peasantry. In assessing the scope and the effectiveness of the late medieval state it is obviously necessary to remember this great mass of mundane business carried through without incident in the king's courts, not least because it helps to place in perspective the much smaller body of evidence on the abuse of the criminal law and the general manipulation of the judicial system by the political elite.

Attitudes to Justice: the Gentry and Nobility

It is with the attitudes of the upper orders to the operation of the royal courts that we are inevitably principally concerned here, not least because those attitudes did most to inform the political ideas on justice formulated in the county courts and articulated in parliament. In many ways, the concerns of the elite were exactly those of the peasantry: that justice was protracted and expensive, too easily dictated by the status of the parties and too often perverted by political interests. At this level, however, the public debate on justice also had certain special characteristics. First, there was a strong feeling that the integrity of royal justice was greatly damaged not simply by endemic corruption but by the particular influence of bastard feudalism upon the judiciary and its judgments. Secondly, there was great concern over the king's ability and willingness to compensate for the evident shortcomings of the judicial system by holding the great men of his realm in check. This section will deal with the first of these issues; the second will be picked up and developed in our concluding analysis of the king's particular responsibility for the maintenance of the law.

The practice of manipulating the judicial system to obtain favourable judgments was known to contemporaries as mainten-ance. Maintenance had only been declared an offence against the crown under Edward I, and the political debate that developed around this issue in the following century may have owed less to a supposed increase in corruption and more to a political culture that was less tolerant of a deeply-rooted practice.[28] When the parliamentary commons found an independent political voice in the early fourteenth century, they quickly adopted a hostile stance towards maintenance and tended to attribute the practice not to the classes from which they sprang but to their social and political superiors among the lords. By the 1370s, the commons were making a specific link between the corruption of the judicial system and the practice of livery: that is, the granting of robes, hoods, caps and badges to the members of a nobleman's household and political following. These arguments have often been seen as a notable example of the hypocrisy of the gentry, who themselves benefited so obviously from the devolution of justice under Edward III and his successors and from the political and judicial favours gained through membership of baronial affinities. It must also be noted, however, that the debate on maintenance was cyclical and that the commons tended to concentrate on the disruptive influence of the magnates at those times when members of the high aristocracy were also in prominent – sometimes violent – political opposition to the crown: as, for example, in the 1320s, the first half of Richard II's reign and the later years of Henry VI. This reminds us that the debate on justice was often less to do with the realities of procedure in the courts and much more to do with general perceptions of the quality of government: in this respect, it is particularly important to realise that the vocabulary of politics itself was firmly rooted in the language and imagery of justice.[29]

If contemporaries were sufficiently sensitive to this discourse to realise that the association of livery and maintenance was something of a construct, it is also clear that political considerations sometimes made it useful for the crown to play on the commons' prejudices and off-load responsibility for the shortcomings of the judicial system onto the high aristocracy. One of the most striking examples of such manoeuvring occurs in the context of Richard II's reaction against his baronial opponents.[30] In the Cambridge Parliament of 1388, the commons demanded the eradication of maintenance, suggesting that the best way to achieve this would be through the abolition of livery. The king appears to have seen this as an opportunity to discredit the magnates – more specifically, the members of the Appellant regime who had recently defied and humiliated him – and to win the confidence of the gentry by making a stand on law and order. In 1389 Richard issued a new set of peace commissions, appointing a large number of new men and completely excluding members of the nobility from their normal position as presidents of the bench. In the following year, he issued a proclamation prohibiting anyone of the rank of knight or below from granting livery and allowing the peerage to bestow it only on household servants and knights and esquires retained for life under formal written contracts. This populist strategy (apparently given enthusiastic support by Geoffrey Chaucer) was an important part of the programme of personal rehabilitation launched by Richard II in 1389–90, and demonstrates with dramatic clarity how judicial policy and legislation could be profoundly influenced by, not to say subordinated to, the political priorities of the crown.

In attempting to assess the impact of these Ricardian initiatives, it is necessary to draw something of a distinction between the central and the local courts. It has been argued that the particular intensity of the debate over justice in the 1380s probably did help to reduce the more blatant abuse of justice in the king's bench and common pleas.[31] The murder of Chief Justice Cavendish in 1381 and the execution of Chief Justice Tresilian by the Appellants in 1388 impressed upon their successors the real hazards they faced from implication both in judicial corruption and in political controversy. Certainly, by the early fifteenth century it was very rare for the king's justices and serjeants to be formally retained by members of the secular and ecclesiastical hierarchy. Nor, interestingly, did such officials now generally fall victim to political reaction: whereas both Edward III in 1340 and the Appellants in 1388 had dismissed and hounded most of the senior judges for their supposed betrayal of the relevant regimes, the staff of the king's bench and common pleas remained very largely untouched by further upheavals until the revolution of 1461. It is also possible that Henry V's decision to make the court of king's bench the centrepiece of his programme for the restoration of law and order in the 1410s gave it, as well as Henry, a lasting reputation for providing more effective and equitable justice. At this level, then, the polity may indeed have begun to perceive an improvement in the quality of justice during the early fifteenth century.

At the local level, by contrast, there can be little doubt that Richard II's attempts to break the magnates' influence in the judicial system failed almost completely. Noblemen soon began to appear once again on the commissions of the peace; and the ordinance of 1390 remained a dead letter. That Richard had been driven by political considerations rather than a real desire to improve the standards of justice was demonstrated clearly in 1397, when he packed a new set of peace commissions with his own supporters among the *duketti* and the members of the royal affinity in the shires.[32] Nor, in a general sense, did the deposition of 1399 greatly alter the situation. The Ricardian legislation on livery was taken up by Henry IV in 1399 – again as a means of winning over the commons – and further extended in a statute of 1406. In theory, this ought to have radically reduced the formal links between lords and judges. In practice, as the various enforcement efforts of all three Lancastrian kings indicate, such legislation could never eradicate the operation and impact of retaining and was only really useful as a symbolic gesture and, on occasions, as a means of persecuting political enemies.[33] The transformative effect of Henry V's judicial policies on popular and political perceptions of royal justice are not to be minimised, and will be discussed below. In the present context, however, we must pursue the continuing concern of the parliamentary commons with the operation of justice and the disruptive influence of the magnates to its conclusion in the mid-fifteenth century.

The basic justification for the devolution of judicial authority to the shires – that local men were best placed to deal with law and order – had itself been called into question by the debate on maintenance and the suggestion that the justices of the peace acted simply as the cronies of the magnates. In continuing to support the principle of devolution underpinning the peace commissions, it was therefore necessary for the commons to emphasise another of their particular preoccupations: namely, that the crown should select as its local agents those men of substance and reputation who were capable of withstanding the pressures brought to bear on them by other members of the local elite. This debate had already resulted under Edward III in the fixing of a property qualification for the offices of escheator and sheriff: that is, the possession of landed income to the value of £20 a year, the level normally regarded as sufficient to support the rank of esquire.[34] But the reform of the quorum on the county bench after 1389, mentioned above, had the effect of increasing the judicial responsibilities of those provincial lawyers who, despite their own aspirations towards gentility, were often men of comparatively modest means and minor political influence.[35] This, coupled with general suspicion about the motives and actions of the men of law who participated in public life, may provide something of the background to the commons' request in 1439–40 for a statute imposing the £20 property qualification on candidates for the peace commissions (though, in the event, the impact of this measure was somewhat blunted by the government's provision that under certain circumstances lawyers without the necessary landed base could still be recruited to the quorum).[36] In other words, then, when the greater gentry presented themselves as the 'best and most sufficient' candidates for local office they did so not simply or even principally to perpetuate an oligarchy but to ensure that government retained the integrity so vital to its stability and continuity.

Consequently, the campaigns of the parliamentary commons against both the magnates' abuse of the legal system and the take-over of local administration by gentlemen-lawyers need not be seen as a mark of the hypocrisy of the gentry but as a statement of the prevailing belief that each order of society had a particular function and public responsibility to fulfil. The gentry now regarded itself as the natural magistracy: indeed, the degree to which landed society came to depend on, and identify with, this role in the century after the Black Death represents one of the most important changes in political culture during the whole of the Middle Ages. The fact that gentility was now particularly associated with service to the state, however, made it vital that all other ranks of society should also honour their own particular public obligations.[37] Above all, the magnates were expected to take the natural lead in showing greater respect for the apparatus and workings of royal justice. If they failed to do this, they were seen to be challenging not only the political but also the rightful social order.

This point helps to explain why the increase in the criminal activity of the nobility and the members of baronial affinities during Henry VI's reign was so much criticised in contemporary political debate. In the 1420s there were already ominous signs of growing aristocratic contempt for the due process of law: Lord Talbot's terrorist activities in Herefordshire are a particular case in point.[38] From the late 1430s feuds between noblemen, or between the members of rival noble retinues, seem increasingly to have degenerated into open violence. One particularly worrying aspect of this development was that it was not confined to those peripheral areas in the south-west, the Welsh marches and the north where a high degree of lawlessness was more or less the norm. At the Bedford quarter sessions in 1439, for instance, a quarrel between two local magnates, Lord Grey of Ruthin and Lord Fanhope, erupted into recriminations, intimidation and thuggery.[39] It is the events in East Anglia, however, that are best known and susceptible of the most dramatic reconstruction: the survival of the *Paston Letters* allows us a unique insight into the way in which William de la Pole mobilised his affinity in Norfolk and Suffolk to ride roughshod over property rights, operate extortion and protection rackets, and either pervert the course of justice or prevent recourse to the law altogether.[40] Neither this example nor the evidence from which it is reconstructed can, of course, be taken as altogether typical. But what gave the case particular prominence in the contemporary political agenda, and what makes it so relevant in the context of the present study, is that de la Pole, the duke of Suffolk, was also Henry VI's greatest ally and closest friend. To criticise the aristocracy for its failure to fulfil social and political obligations was, in this instance, simply to emphasise that the ultimate responsibility for the preservation of order lay with the king.

Kingship, War and Justice

The foregoing discussion ought to have dispelled any lingering suspicion that the devolution of criminal justice during the fourteenth and fifteenth centuries lightened the king's responsibilities as the ultimate guarantor of the law. Indeed, the very success of the peace commissions, not to mention the general increase in civil litigation during the later Middle Ages, made the management of the judicial system a larger and more challenging task than ever before. The question therefore arises as to the relative importance that successive kings gave to the implementation of justice during the period of the long Hundred Years War and the particular techniques they used to persuade the more powerful members of society to observe the proprieties of the law.

There can be little doubt that during the first half of the fourteenth century the administrative and political demands of war with Scotland and France caused the crown increasingly to compromise on its responsibilities for the operation of the law. On the outbreak of hostilities in Gascony in 1294, Edward I called off not only the general eyre but also the *quo warranto* inquiries, another controversial series of local visitations designed specifically to reveal the usurpation of royal rights. For this and succeeding campaigns he also offered a wide range of judicial incentives to those undertaking service as men at arms, including immunity from the assizes and the issue of special commissions of oyer and terminer to investigate violations of rights and property during absences abroad. Much more controversial – not least because it was exploited so extensively by the lower orders who filled up the ranks of the Edwardian infantry – was the flagrant abuse of royal pardons.[41] In return for the performance of military service, both convicted and suspected felons could sue out pardons nullifying the judgments and punishments that had been, or might yet be, passed against them. By the 1330s it was widely believed that the issue of large numbers of pardons was itself provoking a crisis of public order as demobilised soldiers formed themselves into criminal gangs, some of them even led by gentry families such as the notorious Folvilles, and tyrannised certain regions of the country – particularly the midlands – with complete impunity.[42] The situation was bitterly satirised in literature such as the *Song of Trailbaston* and the *Tale of Gamelyn*, where it is the innocent victims of a corrupt judicial system, the outlaws inhabiting the greenwood, who are seen as the only remaining champions of truth and justice. It is even possible that some of the episodes in the Robin Hood ballads can be directly linked to the events and personalities of the 1330s.[43]

What gave the debate on law particular resonance in these years, of course, was the fact that the crown had yet to find an adequate or acceptable agency of law enforcement in the shires. When the peace commissions emerged as a permanent part of the judicial structure, much of the force went out of the political debate – at least, the parliamentary debate – on the way in which war was supposed to have compromised justice. The switch to smaller and more elitist armies raised by voluntary contract in the mid-fourteenth century also greatly reduced the number of pardons issued in return for military service and the criticisms that had earlier surrounded this practice; after some disruption in the 1360s, there is comparatively little evidence of organised criminal activity by quasi-military gangs.[44] It ought perhaps to be added that the personality of the king also had a powerful influence on political perceptions: Edward III's Ordinance of Justices of 1346 and his trial of Chief Justice Thorp in 1350 may have had little real impact on corruption in the courts, but they provided exactly the signals – and the scapegoats – that the polity needed to be assured of the king's good faith.[45] Consequently, the supposed tension between law state and war state, if it ever existed, was very largely resolved to the satisfaction of the contemporary polity (if not to that of all historians) in the period of domestic reconstruction following the Black Death and the treaty of Brétigny.

Among the issues that remained was the enduring tradition that the king's departure from the country on campaign almost inevitably encouraged contempt for the law and led to a deterioration of public order.[46] The vigorous programme of law enforcement undertaken by Henry V as a prelude to his lengthy absences in France was therefore a particularly important element in that king's construction of his public image. Henry's strategy on law and order also provides us with a notable example of the way in which the judicial structure, for all its supposed decentralisation, could still be deployed effectively in the political service of the king. The lollard rising led by Sir John Oldcastle, though a fairly insignificant threat to the throne, justified the imposition of a state of emergency in the Leicester Parliament of 1414. The king's bench, which had rarely moved from Westminster since Edward III's time, was now dispatched to Lichfield and

Shrewsbury where it not only took charge of all criminal business pending in Staffordshire and Shropshire but also acted as a clearing house for cases referred from other subsidiary commissions of inquiry set up in Nottinghamshire, Derbyshire and Yorkshire. Henry had thus set in motion a policy of centralisation in which the king's bench became a kind of 'superior eyre' with powers extending, potentially and ultimately, to every corner of the realm. The abrupt dismantling of this elaborate scheme and the issue of a general pardon to all suspected criminals late in 1414 represented not so much an admission of failure as an acknowledgement of the limitations of the formal judicial system. Henry's brief policy of interventionism had won him a political reputation as the champion of justice; his decision not to proceed with punitive measures did much to reconcile both nobility and commonalty to his regime and secure active support for his ensuing continental campaigns. While the historian might with some justification see this as yet another judicial compromise brought on by a shift to military priorities, it also indicates the delicate balance that had to be struck by all rulers, in peace as well as in war, between the full rigours of royal justice and the need to accommodate the interests and win the confidence of the polity.

Under these circumstances, it is also easy to see why the failure of Henry VI either to resolve disputes between his nobles or to protect the rest of his subjects from aristocratic misrule proved perhaps the most serious defect of an altogether inadequate regime. We have already noted in chapter 4 how the king was expected to act as arbitrator in disputes between his great men and how the collapse of that system in the 1440s contributed to the civil war of the 1450s. In the light of what has been said in this chapter, it ought to be evident that aristocratic feuding was used as an index of lawlessness by the classes represented in the parliamentary commons not simply as a means of disguising the amount of skullduggery in which the gentry also engaged but because the violence and corruption sponsored by the nobility provided the most obvious sign that the king himself was not doing his job properly. It was precisely at the top level of society that the formal judicial structures were effectively inoperable and the whole system rested on the arts of informal political management. For whereas the crown could, and often did, overrule the county benches by sending powerful commissions of oyer and terminer into the shires to investigate particular outbreaks of disorder, such heavy-handed and intrusive actions were highly unlikely to appeal to the nobility on whose cooperation the whole political system actually depended. This explains why Henry VI's belated efforts to stamp his authority on the realm in the wake of the crisis of 1450 were only partly successful. The king's judicial perambulations through the regions in the south-east and south-west that had recently risen in revolt against his government undoubtedly did much to restore the credibility of the Lancastrian monarchy among many members of the polity. But the oyer and terminer sessions held in East Anglia were only partly successful in breaking the following of the toppled duke of Suffolk, and a party led by de la Pole's former henchman, Sir Thomas Tuddenham, survived to vie for power with the equally unscrupulous retainers of the region's new aristocratic power broker, John Mowbray, duke of Norfolk.[47] The 1440s and 1450s showed that the failure of effective political direction from the centre not only jeopardised the operation of the judicial system and the maintenance of law and order, but thereby destroyed the good governance that was the very *raison d'être* of monarchy.

The foregoing discussion has suggested that the fourteenth and fifteenth centuries witnessed considerable fluctuations in public attitudes towards the operations of justice. In the half-century between the abandonment of the general eyre and the emergence of the justices of the peace, there was widespread criticism of the crown's failure to maintain the law state and devise an adequate structure in which it might operate. The devolution of judicial authority in the second half of the fourteenth century was not so much a political concession by an over-burdened war state as a reaction to the demographic and economic upheavals following the Black Death, when, in their common concern to preserve social and political stability, the crown and the landed classes developed an ambitious system of criminal justice and co-operated closely to ensure its proper enforcement. Far from allowing the crown to shift its priorities away from the law and towards the pursuit of foreign wars, this process ensured that justice remained at the centre of domestic political debate and put a higher premium than ever on the king's ability to manage the judicial system. The efficiency or fairness of justice did not therefore depend primarily on the supposed balance between central and local control. Decentralisation simply revealed that the upper orders of English society could not ultimately be coerced into respecting the rule of law but had to be persuaded of the incidental benefits that would follow in its wake in the form of royal favour and patronage. It was this common theme, and the particular emphasis it placed on direction from above, that allowed provincial communities to transcend merely local issues and to articulate their joint concerns over justice at the national level in the political agenda of the parliamentary commons.

7

POLITICAL LIFE

At the end of this study of late medieval English politics, it is time to step back from the details and draw some general conclusions out of the issues and ideas that have emerged. Politics had many dimensions in the later Middle Ages, and this short book cannot pretend to have covered more than a few of them. Its specific purpose has been to trace the existence and concerns of a polity at once constructed from individual local and provincial societies and capable of developing a coherent identity and programme at the national level. We may now proceed to summarise the anatomy of this political society and the resulting temper of late medieval politics and to ask whether the new confidence and power enjoyed by its subjects served to emasculate the late medieval state and cause the Wars of the Roses.

Historians of the gentry often tend to think of the 'political community' only in terms of the 'governing classes' and see the later Middle Ages as the period in which the squirearchy really established its control over the state by taking on the function of a magistracy. But by distinguishing between governance (the active and legitimate exercise of social control) and politics (the public debate surrounding that practice), it has been possible to suggest that the period 1300–1450 also witnessed the development of a broader and more disparate political community. In other words, although the dividing line between the governors and the governed may have denoted the limits of public authority, it did not create a monopoly of influence. Fifteenth-century commentators still inevitably liked to think in terms of a tripartite society of lords (the secular rulers), clergy (the guardians of the spiritual) and labourers (the passive majority), but the changes in both the rural and the urban economies during the century following the Black Death created many new groupings – merchants, gentlemen-lawyers, yeomen farmers and so on – that could not easily be accommodated in this simplistic scheme and which challenged, even if usually only implicitly, the notion that political influence rested exculsively in the traditional elite.[1] The defeat of the Peasants' Revolt was in some senses a decisive blow to the vision of a fully inclusive polity, but the events of 1381 also did something to discredit the exclusive and coercive system of government that had emerged since the Black Death and forced the upper levels of the polity to recognise that the essence of successful administration and justice lay in co-operation.

The most important, because the most effective, forum for national politics in the fourteenth and first half of the fifteenth centuries was parliament. The emergence of the commons under Edward I and Edward III allowed the shire and borough communities for the first time to find a recognised voice in high politics and to make common cause on the issues of general concern to the polity. Since the commons were themselves members of the governing classes, it is easy to suppose that they spoke not for the generality but for the few and that the political grievances of the lesser orders were heard only at the level of the vill, the hundred and, under certain circumstances, the shire. In fact, while acknowledging that the upper reaches of the political structure were heavily weighted in favour of the elite and that their concerns often discriminated against the lower orders, we must note that in some respects the political agenda of the parliamentary commons also had the effect, either deliberately or accidentally, of protecting the peasantry from the full severities of the state.

In particular, the commons' general determination to restrict royal taxation during the period of the long Hundred Years War eventually benefited all the inhabitants of the realm. Before the plague, the knights and burgesses vigorously criticised the crown's fiscal policies for their harmful effects on the poor. This need not, of course, be taken as altruism, for the lesser landholders repre- sented in the commons were naturally anxious to ensure that the rural population should be left with sufficient resources to meet the demands of their feudal lords. Nevertheless, the return to this critical and cautious attitude in the years after the Peasants' Revolt and the ossification of the system of direct taxation had very important consequences for the economic well-being of the peas- antry. Whereas the French monarchy in the late fourteenth and fifteenth centuries was able to use the decline of seigneurial dues as an opportunity vastly to increase its fiscal demands on the peas- antry, in England the state failed almost completely to exploit the new-found prosperity either of the yeomanry or of the labouring classes and had to content itself with taking a small and dwindling proportion of agricultural wealth.[2] These economic benefits may have been largely incidental to the commons' primary aim of defending their *political* right to act as the arbiters of taxation (it was in a specifically fiscal context, after all, that Fortescue argued the difference between the tyranny of the French monarchy and the constitutionality of the English),[3] but it stood as a striking demon- stration of the utility and the real benefits that were provided by the dialogue between crown and community in parliament.

How, then, did political society perceive the 'good governance' that it so constantly demanded of the late medieval crown? Not, apparently, in terms of empire-building. There is no shortage of contemporary comment on the legitimacy and advisability of Edward III's and Henry V's ambitions to fulfil their natural desti- nies in France, but the idea that the realm as a whole benefited from such foreign adventures was largely a construct of royal propaganda and an illusion perpetuated by the military aristocracy and mercantile interest; under Henry VI at least, many members of the polity were probably prepared to admit in private that the war state was indeed a distraction from the major issues facing the domestic regime. Good governance only accommodated warfare, then, when the latter was seen as sustainable and productive. This is not to say, however, that war did not provide the essential context for many of the fundamental political issues of the fourteenth and first half of the fifteenth centuries: without the Hundred Years War, domestic politics and government would surely have had an altogether different character. This is true, above all, of the debate over the public financing of the state. Particularly after the Peasants' Revolt there was considerable and often rather nervous discussion of the king's duty to protect the economic welfare of his subjects and avoid oppressing them with onerous taxes; this, as George Ashby significantly noted in the 1450s in his *Active Policy of a Prince*, was the only real way of persuading the people away from lawlessness and rebellion.[4] Clearly, the tax revolt of 1381 and the challenge it presented to public authority had an enduring impression on all levels of the polity and provides an important explanation for the waning of England's financial commitment to the Hundred Years War during the first half of the fifteenth century.

For the domestic political community gathered in its formal and public assemblies, however, there is little doubt that the heart of 'good governance' lay not in the capacity of kings to mobilise armies and win battles in foreign wars, impressive though these achievements were, but in the preservation of domestic order. Indeed, in the political rhetoric of the later fourteenth and first half of the fifteenth centuries, prosperity itself was often measured in terms not of money but of justice. The demand for 'good and *abundant* governance' (my italics) made in the parliament of 1406 was obviously not a general appeal for greater state intervention but a request for the kind of active political leadership that alone ensured the stability of society.[5] Similarly, the commons in the parliaments of 1449–50 found it natural to express Henry VI's failure to guarantee justice as a political betrayal that jeopardised both the 'wealth' of the king and the 'prosperity' of his subjects.[6] The demand for justice therefore encompassed not simply a concern about the pursuit and prosecution of criminals but a general plea for free access to the remedies supplied by the state and a guarantee that the crown's judgments would prevail and work to the general good. Given the fact that the king ultimately lacked coercive power – neither the law state nor the war state was a police state – it is somewhat difficult for the modern mind to grapple with this debate: perhaps good governance was indeed a naive expectation and an unattainable goal. But contemporaries had no doubt that the answer to this challenge rested in the actions of the king – in the taking of good and wise counsel, the judicious use of the royal prerogative, the effective deployment of patronage as a means of managing the magnates and the general monitoring of the administrative and judicial structures operating in the localities. Ironically and significantly, the shift from a king-centred to a polity-centred analysis advocated at the beginning of this study serves simply to reinforce the extraordinarily high degree to which the system of government in later medieval England depended on the personal record of the ruler.

It is easy to conclude from this, as McFarlane did, that the Wars of the Roses were the consequence of one man's inanity and insanity:[7] the descent into civil war in the later 1450s and the revolution of 1461 can thus be conveniently blamed on Henry VI and the way cleared for the story of the restoration of royal authority under Edward IV and – after the further dynastic disruptions of 1483–5 – the Tudors. This, however, is not an altogether satisfactory or sufficient explanation of the process by which a monarchy that is usually assumed to have reached the height of its medieval powers under Edward I was driven over the following 150 years into compromises and concessions that not only prevented the onward march of the centralised state but fundamentally weakened the institution of the crown and precipitated its *dénouement* in the mid-fifteenth century. It can be argued that it was actually impossible for Henry VI to answer the call for effective leadership because the polity itself had hedged the crown about with so many restrictions that no amount of royal charisma could compensate for the power vacuum now existing at the centre. If we accept this argument about structures rather than personalities – and at least some of what has gone before does indeed lead to it – then we have finally to ask at what point the collapse of the Plantagenet system became more or less inevitable.

The three 'structural' explanations that are normally given among the long-term causes of the Wars of the Roses are: the development of bastard feudalism, which gave members of the aristocracy powerful political followings capable of being mobilised as private armies; the collapse of public order, resulting partly from the influence of bastard feudalism and partly from the devolution of the judicial system; and the longevity, expense and ultimate defeat of the English in the Hundred Years War, which drove the crown into political compromises and financial bankruptcy. (A fourth possible explanation, the supposed influence of the royal depositions of 1327 and 1399, is now very much played down for reasons already discussed in Chapter 4.) Not surprisingly, it is in the reign of Edward III, when all three of these issues came to the fore, that many historians have traced the decisive shift of initiative from crown to aristocracy and polity or, as it is often now expressed, from centre to locality. The devolution of the tax system and of criminal justice during this reign undoubtedly speak much for the new administrative priorities and political balance necessitated by the wars in France; it is also possible that the omission of private war from the definition of high treason provided in the statute of 1352 signalled a degree of royal leniency towards aristocratic unruliness that would cause substantial problems for Edward's successors. Edward III was a pragmatist, disinclined to grand statements of royal authority and more inclined to seek effective working relationships both with his nobles and with the wider political community. The search for such an accommodation undeniably entailed both constitutional adjustments and – if only in hindsight – high political risks.

Nevertheless, two important qualifications need perhaps to be registered at this point. Firstly, the character of government had already begun to change as soon as Edward I chose to make war against Scotland and France in the 1290s: the reactive nature of Edward III's regime, signified by the absence of major government-inspired law codes and the general take-over of the legislative process by parliament, was in fact only the continuation of a trend begun under his mighty grandfather.[8] Secondly, it is not at all certain that this general trend was necessarily irreversible. Had Edward III got the diplomatic settlement he was offered in 1360 – namely, sovereign control over the duchy of Aquitaine in return for his own renunciation of the French throne – then both the war and its associated burdens would have ended. The emergency administrative and judicial measures adopted during the middle decades of the fourteenth century would then have been reviewed and the king might well have capitalised on his diplomatic success by re-establishing a more centralised and authoritarian form of government. The tax experiments of the 1370s and the withdrawal of the determining powers of the commissions of the peace in the 1360s and the 1380s certainly indicate the degree of flexibility that still existed in the structure of royal administration, while Richard II's experiments with a new kind of government during the years of peace in the 1390s – and particularly his development of a royal affinity – did much to alter the perceived balance between centre and locality. There are also signs that Richard intended to reconstruct the function and authority of the crown by re-defining and actively exercising the royal prerogative. In assessing Richard II's contribution to the fate of the English monarchy, we certainly have to be careful to distinguish between the creative political novelties of his regime and the unacceptable tyrannical behaviour of the late 1390s that brought about his demise.

If there was a particular point at which the crown lost the initiative in government, then, it came not necessarily in the fourteenth century, nor at the change of dynasty in 1399, but under that apparent exemplar of late medieval monarchy, Henry V. This suggestion is made not with the intention of being deliberately perverse, but in order to emphasise the political opportunities missed during the period of euphoria following the battle of Agincourt and the constitutional challenges raised by the Troyes settlement of 1420. The modern adulation of Henry V rests almost completely on his ability to mobilise the existing administrative, fiscal and judicial structures and make them work more effectively; that certain of those structures were themselves in urgent need of fundamental reform is a point that remarkably few historians seem prepared to admit. The law and order initiative of 1414, discussed in the previous chapter, depended entirely on the redeployment of existing judicial agencies, and was of only brief duration. Above all, however, Henry's reluctance or inability to undertake far-reaching reforms of the fiscal and financial systems had a devastating impact on his successor's regime. The intense political problems experienced by Henry VI's regime in the closing stages of the French war arose not simply from the decline in revenue from taxation and the growth of the king's debts from an estimated £168,000 in 1433 to a crippling £372,000 in 1450, but also from the unrealistically high standards that Henry V himself had set in the management of finance and the particular import- ance he had attached to the repayment of royal creditors: unlike his predecessors in the fourteenth century, Henry VI simply lacked the freedom to renege on his debts.[9] By failing to create a new fiscal infrastructure that would allow his successor to fulfil the new standards of financial rectitude that he had added to the public notion of good governance, Henry V may indeed be said to have contributed directly, even decisively, to the bankruptcy of the Lancastrian regime.

Finally, and in contrast to Edward III's treaty of Brétigny, the diplomatic settlement worked out by Henry V in 1420 was an agenda not so much for peace as for war – and war, indeed, on a grand scale. Even if Henry had lived to old age, the dual monarchy envisioned in the treaty of Troyes could not have been effected without further major military commitments in France; and the resulting financial exactions and political turmoil that would necessarily have been experienced in England would have made it more or less impossible, even without the additional complication of a minority administration, for the crown to re-establish the political initiative and undertake far-reaching changes in the struc- ture of government. The diplomatic settlement of 1420 therefore effectively postponed the possibility of reformist and intervention- ist monarchy and the restoration of the state until the war that it had created was itself over. To say that the end of the Hundred Years War inevitably meant the beginning of the Wars of the Roses is not only to impose anachronistic labels and unfashionable ideas of causality but also to ignore the extraordinary complexity of domestic politics in the 1450s.[10] But to argue that the later stages of the Anglo-French wars created irresolvable dilemmas for both the crown *and* the political community is simply to confirm that the military and diplomatic ambitions of the monarchy did indeed represent one of the primary conditioning forces in English politi- cal life throughout the period from 1300 to 1450.[11]

137

NOTES

Abbreviations Used in the Notes

BIHR	*Bulletin of the Institute of Historical Research*
EHD 3	H. Rothwell (ed.), *English Historical Documents III: 1189–1327* (London: Eyre & Spottiswoode, 1975)
EHD 4	A. R. Myers (ed.), *English Historical Documents IV: 1327–1485* (London: Eyre & Spottiswoode, 1969)
EHR	*English Historical Review*
JBS	*Journal of British Studies*
P&P	*Past and Present*
TRHS	*Transactions of the Royal Historical Society*

1 POLITICAL SOCIETY AND POLITICAL EVENTS

1. See, for example, the prominence of English examples in J.-P. Genet, 'L'état moderne: un modèle opératoire?', in J.-P. Genet (ed.), *L'état moderne: genèse* (Paris: Éditions du CNRS, 1990) pp. 261–81.
2. The implications are discussed in a form relevant to the theme of this book by S. J. Payling, 'Social Mobility, Demographic Change, and Landed Society in Late Medieval England', *Economic History Review*, 2nd series 45 (1992) pp. 51–73.
3. That is, those (excluding the baronage) assessed in 1436 as having landed income in excess of £10 per annum: see H. L. Gray, 'Incomes from Land in England in 1436', *EHR*, 49 (1934) pp. 607–31, esp. p. 630.

Note that Gray's figures include extrapolations to compensate for missing data.

4. J. P. Cooper, *Land, Men and Beliefs* (London: Hambledon Press, 1984) pp. 43–77, esp. p. 43; D. A. L. Morgan, 'The Individual Style of the English Gentleman', in M. Jones (ed.), *Gentry and Lesser Nobility in Late Medieval Europe* (Gloucester: Alan Sutton, 1984) pp. 15–35.

5. For what follows, see R. Horrox, 'The Urban Gentry in the Fifteenth Century', in J. A. F. Thomson (ed.), *Towns and Townspeople in the Fifteenth Century* (Gloucester: Alan Sutton, 1988) pp. 22–44; R. Horrox, *The de la Poles of Hull*, East Yorkshire Local History Series 38 (Beverley, 1983); S. O'Connor, 'Adam Fraunceys and Adam Pyel', in D. J. Clayton, R. G. Davies and P. McNiven (eds), *Trade, Devotion and Governance* (Stroud: Alan Sutton, 1994) pp. 17–35.

6. For what follows, see N. Ramsay, 'What was the Legal Profession?', and B. Vale, 'The Profits of the Law and the "Rise" of the Scropes', in M. Hicks (ed.), *Profit, Piety and the Professions in Later Medieval England* (Gloucester: Alan Sutton, 1990) pp. 62–71, 91–102.

7. For what follows, see A. Macfarlane, *The Origins of English Individualism* (Oxford: Basil Blackwell, 1978); N. Saul, 'The Social Status of Chaucer's Franklin: a Reconsideration', *Medium Aevum*, 52 (1983) 10–26; C. E. Moreton, 'A Social Gulf? The Upper and Lesser Gentry of Later Medieval England', *Journal of Medieval History*, 17 (1991) pp. 255–62; C. Richmond, *The Paston Family in the Fifteenth Century: The First Phase* (Cambridge: Cambridge University Press, 1990).

8. R. B. Dobson (ed.), *The Peasants' Revolt of 1381*, 2nd edn (London: Macmillan, 1983) pp. 106–11.

9. Gray, 'Incomes from Land', p. 630.

10. R. B. Goheen, 'Peasant Politics? Village Communities and the Crown in Fifteenth-Century England', *American Historical Review*, 96 (1991) pp. 42–62; C. Carpenter, 'Law, Justice and Landowners in Late Medieval England', *Law and History Review*, 1 (1983) p. 217; J. Coleman, *English Literature in History, 1350–1400* (London: Hutchinson, 1981) pp. 58–156.

11. J. S. Hamilton, *Piers Gaveston Earl of Cornwall* (Detroit: Wayne State University Press, 1988) pp. 16–17, 109–12; P. Chaplais, *Piers Gaveston: Edward II's Adoptive Brother* (Oxford: Clarendon Press, 1994) pp. 6–13, 113–14.

12. C. M. Barron, 'The Tyranny of Richard II', *BIHR*, 41 (1968) pp. 1–18. Note, however, the rather different perspectives recently adopted by the same author: 'The Deposition of Richard II', in J. Taylor and W. Childs (eds), *Politics and Crisis in Fourteenth-Century England* (Gloucester: Alan Sutton, 1990) pp. 132–49.

13. M. Aston, 'Lollardy and Sedition', in R. H. Hilton (ed.), *Peasants, Knights*

and Heretics (Cambridge: Cambridge University Press, 1976) pp. 303–10, 316–18; R. A. Griffiths, *The Reign of King Henry VI* (London: Ernest Benn, 1981) pp. 139–40.

14. Cf K. B. McFarlane, *The Nobility of Later Medieval England* (Oxford: Clarendon Press, 1973) pp. 120–1; K. B. McFarlane, *England in the Fifteenth Century* (London: Hambledon Press, 1981) pp. 42, 238–9.

15. M. Bentley, 'The British State and its Historiography', in W. Blockmans and J.-P. Genet (eds), *Visions sur le développement des états européens: théories et historiographies de l'état moderne* (Rome: École française de Rome, 1993) pp. 153–68.

16. C. Richmond, 'After McFarlane', *History*, 68 (1983) pp. 46–60.

2 POLITICAL INSTITUTIONS: THE CENTRE

1. The earlier historiography and the revisionism are summarised in M. C. Buck, 'The Reform of the Exchequer, 1316–1326', *EHR*, 98 (1983) pp. 241–3.

2. D. Starkey, 'The Age of the Household', in S. Medcalf (ed.), *The Context of English Literature* (London: Methuen, 1981) pp. 225–90.

3. See the example cited by R. I. Jack, 'Entail and Descent: the Hastings Inheritance', *BIHR*, 38 (1965) p. 6.

4. N. Fryde, *The Tyranny and Fall of Edward II* (Cambridge: Cambridge University Press, 1979) p. 47.

5. W. M. Ormrod, *The Reign of Edward III* (London and New Haven: Yale University Press, 1990) p. 118 and n. 142; K. B. McFarlane, *The Nobility of Later Medieval England* (Oxford: Clarendon Press, 1973) p. 232.

6. J. L. Kirby (ed.), *Calendar of Signet Letters of Henry IV and Henry V* (London: HMSO, 1978) pp. 2–3.

7. For the role of the court in directing provincial culture, see V. J. Scattergood and J. W. Sherborne (eds), *English Court Culture in the Later Middle Ages* (London: Duckworth, 1983).

8. C. Given-Wilson, 'The King and the Gentry in Fourteenth-century England', *TRHS*, 5th series 37 (1987) pp. 97–8.

9. R. A. Griffiths, 'Public and Private Bureaucracies in England and Wales in the Fifteenth Century', *TRHS*, 5th series 30 (1980) pp. 109–30. C. Given-Wilson, *The Royal Household and the King's Affinity* (London and New Haven: Yale University Press, 1986) p. 245, argues against McFarlane's thesis that Henry V attempted to secure the undivided loyalty of his annuitants. See also G. L. Harriss, 'Financial Policy', in G. L. Harriss (ed.), *Henry V: The Practice of Kingship* (Oxford: Oxford University Press, 1985) pp. 173–4.

10. The balance is nicely judged by R. F. Green, *Poets and Princepleasers* (Toronto: University of Toronto Press, 1980) pp. 27–8.

11. C. L. Kingsford, 'Historical Notes on Medieval London Houses', *London Topographical Record*, 10 (1916) pp. 44–144; 12 (1920) pp. 1–66.

12. C. Given-Wilson, 'Royal Charter Witness Lists, 1327–1399', *Medieval Prosopography*, 12, no. 2 (1991) pp. 35–94; J. Catto, 'The King's Servants', in Harriss (ed.), *Henry V*, pp. 88–9. Given-Wilson sees the charter witness lists as evidence of participation in the council.

13. J. L. Watts, 'Domestic Politics and the Constitution in the Reign of Henry VI, *c.* 1435–61', University of Cambridge Ph.D. thesis (1990) pp. 246–73.

14. See the references cited by P. A. Johnson, *Duke Richard of York* (Oxford: Clarendon Press, 1988) p. 70.

15. *EHD*, 3, pp. 527–39.

16. It should be stressed, however, that the contexts were rather different: see J. G. Edwards, '"Justice" in Early English Parliaments', in E. B. Fryde and E. Miller (eds), *Historical Studies of the English Parliament* (Cambridge: Cambridge University Press, 1970) vol. 1, pp. 279–97.

17. G. O. Sayles, *The Functions of the Medieval Parliament of England* (London: Hambledon Press, 1988) pp. 423–4.

18. J. F. Baldwin, 'The King's Council', in J. F. Willard *et al.* (eds), *The English Government at Work 1327–1336* (Cambridge, MA: Medieval Academy of America, 1940–50) vol. 1, pp. 129–39.

19. N. B. Lewis, 'The Continual Council in the Early Years of Richard II', *EHR*, 41 (1926) pp. 246–51; T. F. Tout, *Chapters in the Administrative History of Mediaeval England* (Manchester: Manchester University Press, 1920–33) vol. 3, pp. 326–50.

20. Tout, *Chapters*, vol. 3, p. 454.

21. A. L. Brown, 'The Commons and the Council in the Reign of Henry IV', in Fryde and Miller (eds), *Historical Studies*, vol. 2, pp. 31–60.

22. P. McNiven, 'The Problem of Henry IV's Health', *EHR*, 100 (1985) pp. 747–72.

23. J. L. Kirby, 'Councils and Councillors of Henry IV', *TRHS*, 5th series 14 (1964) pp. 35–65; Catto, 'The King's Servants', pp. 88–9.

24. A. L. Brown, 'The King's Councillors in Fifteenth-century England', *TRHS*, 5th series 19 (1969) pp. 107–8.

25. Watts, 'Domestic Politics', pp. 138–219; J. L. Watts, 'The Counsels of King Henry VI, *c.* 1435–1445', *EHR*, 106 (1991) pp. 279–98.

26. R. A. Griffiths, 'The King's Council and the First Protectorate of the Duke of York', *EHR*, 99 (1984) pp. 67–82; Johnson, *Duke Richard of York*, pp. 126–37.

27. For a powerful corrective, see S. Reynolds, *Kingdoms and Communities in Western Europe, 900–1300* (Oxford: Clarendon Press, 1984).
28. N. Pronay and J. Taylor (eds), *Parliamentary Texts of the Later Middle Ages* (Oxford: Clarendon Press, 1980) pp. 67–70, 80–2.
29. H. G. Richardson and G. O. Sayles, *The English Parliament in the Middle Ages* (London: Hambledon Press, 1981) chapters VI, XVII, XXII.
30. J. S. Roskell, 'The Problem of the Attendance of the Lords in Medieval Parliaments', *BIHR*, 29 (1956) pp. 153–204.
31. A. L. Brown, 'Parliament, *c.* 1377–1422', in R. G. Davies and J. H. Denton (eds), *The English Parliament in the Middle Ages* (Manchester: Manchester University Press, 1981) pp. 132, 138–9.
32. G. L. Harriss, *King, Parliament and Public Finance in Medieval England to 1369* (Oxford: Clarendon Press, 1975) pp. 233–4, 319–20; Ormrod, *Reign of Edward III*, pp. 63–4, 168; Brown, 'Parliament, *c.* 1377–1422', pp. 138–9.
33. This deliberately skirts over the substantial debate on the meaning of consent summarised by M. Prestwich, *English Politics in the Thirteenth Century* (Basingstoke: Macmillan, 1990) pp. 109–28.
34. Ibid., pp. 129–45, provides a convenient summary.
35. Pronay and Taylor (eds), *Parliamentary Texts*, pp. 77, 89–90.
36. For their offer in 1339–40, which implicated the villeins on their own demesnes, see Harriss, *King, Parliament*, pp. 255–8. The income tax of 1404 had a very different catchment: see J. L. Kirby, *Henry IV of England* (London: Constable, 1970) p. 175.
37. Brown, 'Parliament, *c.* 1377–1422', p. 125.
38. For what follows see J. R. Maddicott, 'Parliament and the Constituencies, 1272–1377', in Davies and Denton (eds), *English Parliament*, pp. 61–87.
39. Ormrod, *Reign of Edward III*, pp. 57–8; A. R. Myers, 'Parliamentary Petitions in the Fifteenth Century', *EHR*, 52 (1937) p. 389; P. Wormald, '*Lex scripta* and *verbum regis*', in P. H. Sawyer and I. N. Woods (eds), *Early Medieval Kingship* (Leeds: University of Leeds, 1977) p. 113.
40. F. M. Powicke, *The Thirteenth Century*, 2nd edn (Oxford: Clarendon Press, 1962) p. 704 and n. 1.
41. W. M. Ormrod, 'Agenda for Legislation, 1322–*c.* 1340', *EHR*, 105 (1990) pp. 1–33.
42. W. R. Jones, 'Bishops, Politics and the Two Laws', *Speculum*, 51 (1966) pp. 209–45; Ormrod, *Reign of Edward III*, pp. 139–43.
43. D. Rayner, 'The Forms and Machinery of the "Commune Petition" in the Fourteenth Century', *EHR*, 56 (1941) pp. 213–15; M. McKisack, *The Fourteenth Century* (Oxford: Clarendon Press, 1959) p. 477. For the free speech issue raised by this case, see J. S. Roskell, 'The Parliamentary

Privileges of the Commons', in J. S. Roskell, L. Clark and C. Rawcliffe, *The House of Commons, 1386–1421* (Stroud: Alan Sutton, 1992) vol. 1, pp. 155–6.

44. G. L. Harriss, 'The Commons' Petition of 1340', *EHR*, 78 (1963) pp. 625–54; Harriss, *King, Parliament*, pp. 257–8, 365–75, 502–8.

45. G. Holmes, *The Good Parliament* (Oxford: Clarendon Press, 1975) p. 196; A. Rogers, 'Henry IV, the Commons and Taxation', *Mediaeval Studies*, 31 (1969) p. 44; R. A. Griffiths, *The Reign of King Henry VI* (London: Ernest Benn, 1981) p. 380.

46. T. F. T. Plucknett, *Statutes and their Interpretation in the First Half of the Fourteenth Century* (Cambridge: Cambridge University Press, 1922).

47. Myers, 'Parliamentary Petitions', pp. 590–613.

3 POLITICAL IDENTITIES: THE LOCALITIES

1. R. B. Goheen, 'Peasant Politics? Village Communities and the Crown in Fifteenth-century England', *American Historical Review*, 96 (1991) p. 47.

2. R. H. Hilton, *The English Peasantry in the Later Middle Ages* (Oxford: Clarendon Press, 1975) pp. 20–36; R. H. Hilton, *Class Conflict and the Crisis of Feudalism*, 2nd edn (London: Verso, 1990) pp. 49–65.

3. R. Faith, 'The "Great Rumour" of 1377 and Peasant Ideology', in R. H. Hilton and T. H. Aston (eds), *The English Rising of 1381* (Cambridge: Cambridge University Press, 1984) pp. 43–73.

4. R. B. Dobson (ed.), *The Peasants' Revolt of 1381*, 2nd edn (London: Macmillan, 1983) pp. 254–6; N. Brooks, 'The Organization and Achievements of the Peasants of Kent and Essex in 1381', in H. Mayr-Harting and R. I. Moore (eds), *Studies in Medieval History Presented to R. H. C. Davies* (London: Hambledon Press, 1985) pp. 247–70. Compare A. Prescott, 'London in the Peasants' Revolt', *London Journal*, 7 (1981) pp. 125–43.

5. J. A. Tuck, 'Nobles, Commons and the Great Revolt of 1381', in Hilton and Aston (eds), *English Rising*, pp. 209–10.

6. Goheen, 'Peasant Politics?', pp. 58–9; R. H. Hilton, *The Decline of Serfdom in Medieval England*, 2nd edn (Cambridge: Cambridge University Press, 1983) pp. 47–8.

7. For which see J. R. Maddicott, 'Parliament and the Constituencies, 1272–1377', in R. G. Davies and J. H. Denton (eds), *The English Parliament in the Middle Ages* (Manchester: Manchester University Press, 1981) pp. 62–9.

8. W. M. Ormrod, 'The Crown and the English Economy, 1290–1348', in B. M. S. Campbell (ed.), *Before the Black Death* (Manchester: Manchester University Press, 1991) p. 157.

9. For what follows see J. R. Maddicott, 'The County Community and the

Making of Public Opinion in Fourteenth-century England', *TRHS*, 5th series 28 (1978) pp. 27–43. It should be noted that Maddicott's thesis is not universally accepted: see R. C. Palmer, *The County Courts of Medieval England* (Princeton, NJ: Princeton University Press, 1982).

10. See, e.g., A. Rogers, 'The Lincolnshire County Court in the Fifteenth Century', *Lincolnshire History and Archaeology*, 1 (1966) pp. 64–78.

11. For what follows, see S. J. Payling, 'The Widening Franchise', in D. Williams (ed.), *England in the Fifteenth Century* (Woodbridge: Boydell Press, 1987) pp. 167–85, and the sources cited there.

12. M. James, 'Ritual, Drama and the Social Body in the Late Medieval English Town', *P&P*, 98 (1983) pp. 3–29.

13. S. Rigby, 'Urban "Oligarchy" in Late Medieval England', in J. A. F. Thomson (ed.), *Towns and Townspeople in the Fifteenth Century* (Gloucester: Alan Sutton, 1988) pp. 62–86.

14. A. F. Butcher, 'English Urban Society and the Revolt of 1381', in Hilton and Aston (eds), *English Rising*, pp. 84–111.

15. D. M. Palliser, 'Urban Decay Revisited', in Thomson (ed.), *Towns and Townspeople*, p. 4.

16. M. McKisack, *The Parliamentary Representation of the English Boroughs during the Middle Ages* (Oxford: Clarendon Press, 1932); R. Horrox, 'Urban Patronage and Patrons in the Fifteenth Century', in R. A. Griffiths (ed.), *Patronage, the Crown and the Provinces in Later Medieval England* (Gloucester: Alan Sutton, 1981) pp. 145–66.

17. Maddicott, 'Parliament and the Constituencies', pp. 69–70, 76–7.

18. C. E. Moreton, 'A Social Gulf? The Upper and Lesser Gentry of Later Medieval England', *Journal of Medieval History*, 17 (1991) pp. 255–62; C. Richmond, *John Hopton* (Cambridge: Cambridge University Press, 1981).

19. T. Turville-Petre, 'Humphrey de Bohun and *William of Palerne*', *Neuphilologische Mitteilungen*, 75 (1974) pp. 250–2; M. J. Bennett, '*Sir Gawain and the Green Knight* and the Literary Achievement of the North-west Midlands', *Journal of Medieval History*, 5 (1979) pp. 63–88.

20. Maddicott, 'County Community', pp. 27–43. For a recent review, see R. Virgoe, 'Aspects of the County Community in the Fifteenth Century', in M. Hicks (ed.), *Profit, Piety and the Professions in Later Medieval England* (Gloucester: Alan Sutton, 1990) pp. 1–13.

21. Maddicott, 'County Community', p. 30.

22. As suggested by C. Carpenter, *Locality and Polity* (Cambridge: Cambridge University Press, 1992) pp. 341–2 and n. 246, with references. For Leicestershire see now also I. Acheson, *A Gentry Community: Leicestershire in the Fifteenth Century* (Cambridge: Cambridge University Press, 1992) pp. 126–7.

23. A. J. Pollard, *North-Eastern England during the Wars of the Roses* (Oxford: Clarendon Press, 1990) p. 153; N. Saul, *Scenes from Provincial Life* (Oxford: Clarendon Press, 1986) p. 58.

24. Maddicott, 'County Community', pp. 41–2.

25. Carpenter, *Locality and Polity*, pp. 267–72, 340–1, with references.

26. P. C. Maddern, *Violence and Social Order* (Oxford: Clarendon Press, 1992) pp. 61–4; S. Payling, *Political Society in Lancastrian England* (Oxford: Clarendon Press, 1991) pp. 174–80; S. Walker, 'Yorkshire Justices of the Peace, 1389–1413', *EHR*, 108 (1993) pp. 281–311.

27. G. L. Harriss, 'Introduction', in K. B. McFarlane, *England in the Fifteenth Century* (London: Hambledon Press, 1981) p. xi; C. Carpenter, 'The Beauchamp Affinity: a Study of Bastard Feudalism at Work', *EHR*, 95 (1980) pp. 513–18.

28. McFarlane, *Fifteenth Century*, pp. 24–8; Carpenter, 'Beauchamp Affinity', p. 519; S. Walker, *The Lancastrian Affinity* (Oxford: Clarendon Press, 1990) pp. 41–2 (the exception that proves the rule); S. L. Waugh, 'Tenure to Contract: Lordship and Clientage in Thirteenth-century England', *EHR*, 101 (1986) pp. 811–39.

29. McFarlane, *Fifteenth Century*, pp. 248–54; A. Goodman, *The Wars of the Roses* (London: Routledge & Kegan Paul, 1981) pp. 127–9.

30. S. K. Walker, 'Lancaster v. Dallingridge', *Sussex Archaeological Collections*, 121 (1983) pp. 87–94, is widely cited in this respect. For a vigorous statement of the position, see Payling, *Political Society*, pp. 87–108.

31. R. Horrox, *Richard III: A Study of Service* (Cambridge: Cambridge University Press, 1989) pp. 1–26.

32. M. J. Bennett, *Community, Class and Careerism* (Cambridge: Cambridge University Press, 1983) pp. 215–23.

33. N. Saul, *Knights and Esquires* (Oxford: Clarendon Press, 1981) pp. 60–105; S. M. Wright, *The Derbyshire Gentry in the Fifteenth Century*, Derbyshire Record Society 8 (Chesterfield, 1983) pp. 60–82; M. Cherry, 'The Courtenay Earls of Devon', *Southern History*, 1 (1979) pp. 71–97; Carpenter, 'Beauchamp Affinity', pp. 513–32. For the limits of this approach, see E. Powell, 'After "After McFarlane"', in D. J. Clayton, R. C. Davies and P. McNiven (eds), *Trade, Devotion and Government* (Stroud: Alan Sutton, 1994) pp. 7–8.

34. E. Powell, 'Arbitration and the Law in England in the late Middle Ages', *TRHS*, 5th series 33 (1983) pp. 49–67.

35. Payling, *Political Society*, pp. 186–215.

36. Carpenter, *Locality and Polity*, pp. 399–400, 437–9.

37. See, most recently, P. R. Coss, 'Bastard Feudalism Revised', *P&P*, 125 (1989) pp. 27–64; P. R. Coss, 'Bastard Feudalism Revised: Reply', *P&P*, 131 (1991) pp. 190–203.

38. N. Saul, 'The Despensers and the Downfall of Edward II', *EHR*, 99 (1984) pp. 1–33; R. Virgoe, 'The Crown, Magnates and Local Government in Fifteenth-century East Anglia', in J. R. L. Highfield and R. Jeffs (eds), *The Crown and Local Communities* (Gloucester: Alan Sutton, 1981) pp. 72–87.

39. S. K. Walker, 'Lordship and Lawlessness in the Palatine of Lancaster, 1370–1400', *JBS*, 28 (1989) pp. 325–48.

40. Maddicott, 'Parliament and the Constituencies', pp. 72–4.

41. G. Holmes, *The Good Parliament* (Oxford: Clarendon Press, 1975) p. 184; C. Given-Wilson (ed.), *Chronicles of the Revolution 1397–1400* (Manchester: Manchester University Press, 1993) p. 178. For the context, see Walker, *Lancastrian Affinity*, pp. 237–40; C. Given-Wilson, *The Royal Household and the King's Affinity* (London and New Haven: Yale University Press, 1986) pp. 246–9.

42. Dobson (ed.), *Peasants' Revolt*, p. 340.

43. M. M. Postan, *The Medieval Economy and Society* (Harmondsworth: Penguin Books, 1975) p. 170; Tuck, 'Nobles, Commons', pp. 194–212.

44. H. J. Hewitt, *The Organization of War under Edward III* (Manchester: Manchester University Press, 1966) pp. 158–68; Maddicott, 'County Community', pp. 34–6; W. R. Jones, 'The English Church and Royal Propaganda during the Hundred Years War', *JBS*, 19, no. 1 (1979) pp. 18–30.

45. Maddicott, 'County Community', pp. 36–7.

46. N. Pronay and J. Taylor (eds), *Parliamentary Texts of the Later Middle Ages* (Oxford: Clarendon Press, 1980) pp. 153–73; T. F. Tout, 'The English Parliament and Public Opinion', in E. B. Fryde and E. Miller (eds), *Historical Studies of the English Parliament* (Cambridge: Cambridge University Press, 1970), vol. 1, pp. 298–315; J. Taylor, 'The Good Parliament and its Sources', in J. Taylor and W. Childs (eds), *Politics and Crisis in Fourteenth-Century England* (Gloucester: Alan Sutton, 1990) pp. 81–96. References to parliaments in other chronicles are listed by H. G. Richardson and G. O. Sayles, *The English Parliament in the Middle Ages* (London: Hambledon Press, 1981) chapters V, XVI, XXI.

47. P. R. Coss, 'Aspects of Cultural Diffusion', *P&P*, 108 (1985) pp. 35–79.

48. J. R. Maddicott, 'Poems of Social Protest in Early Fourteenth Century England', in W. M. Ormrod (ed.), *England in the Fourteenth Century* (Woodbridge: Boydell Press, 1986) pp. 130–44.

49. The vast literature, and the pertinent questions, are summarised in H. Jewell, '*Piers Plowman* – a Poem of Crisis', in Taylor and Childs (eds), *Politics and Crisis*, pp. 59–80; C. M. Barron, 'William Langland: a London Poet', in B. A. Hanawalt (ed.), *Chaucer's England* (Minneapolis: University of Minnesota Press, 1992) pp. 91–109.

50. J. Coleman, *English Literature in History, 1350–1400* (London: Hutchinson, 1981) pp. 117–20.
51. H. Barr (ed.), *The Piers Plowman Tradition* (London: Dent, 1993) pp. 101–33. For discussion, see H. M. Cam, *Liberties and Communities in Medieval England* (London: Merlin Press, 1963) pp. 229–35.
52. S. Crane, 'The Writing Lesson of 1381', in B. A. Hanawalt (ed.), *Chaucer's England* (Minneapolis: University of Minnesota Press, 1992) pp. 211–13.
53. This is the theme of Coleman, *English Literature*. See also E. D. Jones, 'Lancastrian Politics, the French War, and the Rise of the Popular Element', *Speculum*, 58 (1993) pp. 95–138.
54. R. H. Robbins (ed.), *Historical Poems of the XIVth and XVth Centuries* (New York: Columbia University Press, 1959) pp. 102–6; also printed in Dobson (ed.), *Peasants' Revolt*, pp. 88–91.
55. R. M. Haines, '"Our master mariner, our sovereign lord"', *Mediaeval Studies*, 38 (1976) pp. 85–96. For another 'ship of state' poem of 1458 referring only to the roles of named royals and nobles, see Robbins (ed.), *Historical Poems*, pp. 191–3.

4 POLITICAL ISSUES: KINGSHIP

1. E. Venables and A. R. Maddison (eds), *The Chronicle of Louth Park Abbey* (Horncastle: privately printed, 1891) p. 41.
2. *EHD*, 4, pp. 72–3.
3. C. Given-Wilson (ed.), *Chronicles of the Revolution 1397–1400* (Manchester: Manchester University Press, 1993) p. 172.
4. A. Harding, 'The Revolt Against the Justices', in R. H. Hilton and T. H. Aston (eds), *The English Rising of 1381* (Cambridge: Cambridge University Press, 1984) pp. 167–8.
5. A. P. Baldwin, *The Theme of Government in Piers Plowman* (Woodbridge: Boydell Press, 1981); H. Barr (ed.), *The Piers Plowman Tradition* (London: Dent, 1993) pp. 30–5, 205–10.
6. J.-P. Genet, 'Ecclesiastics and Political Theory in Late Medieval England', in B. Dobson (ed.), *The Church, Politics and Patronage in the Fifteenth Century* (Gloucester: Alan Sutton, 1984) pp. 23–44; J.-P. Genet (ed.), *Four Political Tracts of the Later Middle Ages*, Camden Soc., 4th series 18 (London, 1977). See also G. L. Harriss, 'Introduction', in G. L. Harriss (ed.), *Henry V: The Practice of Kingship* (Oxford: Oxford University Press, 1985) pp. 1–29.
7. J. Alexander and P. Binski (eds), *Age of Chivalry* (London: Royal Academy, 1987); J. W. McKenna, 'Henry VI and the Dual Monarchy', *Journal of the Warburg and Courtauld Institutes*, 28 (1965) pp. 145–62.

8. M. Prestwich, 'The Piety of Edward I', in W. M. Ormrod (ed.), *England in the Thirteenth Century* (Woodbridge: Boydell Press, 1985) pp. 125–6; W. M. Ormrod, 'The Personal Religion of Edward III', *Speculum*, 64 (1989) pp. 862–5.

9. R. H. Jones, *The Royal Policy of Richard II* (Oxford: Basil Blackwell, 1968) pp. 125–46.

10. A. Black, *Political Thought in Europe 1250–1450* (Cambridge: Cambridge University Press, 1992) pp. 154–5.

11. J. L. Watts, 'Domestic Politics and the Constitution in the Reign of Henry VI, *c.* 1435–61', University of Cambridge Ph.D. thesis (1990) pp. 52–7.

12. C. Carpenter, *Locality and Polity* (Cambridge: Cambridge University Press, 1992) pp. 3–7, 630–4, with references.

13. W. M. Ormrod, 'Edward III's Government of England, c. 1346–c. 1356', University of Oxford D.Phil. thesis (1984) p. 90; A. L. Brown, 'The Authorization of Letters under the Great Seal', *BIHR*, 37 (1964) pp. 153–4.

14. P. C. Saunders, 'Royal Ecclesiastical Patronage in England, 1199–1351', University of Oxford D.Phil. thesis (1978) pp. 251–4, Appendix I.

15. *EHD*, 3, p. 528.

16. J. J. N. Palmer, 'The Parliament of 1385 and the Constitutional Crisis of 1386', *Speculum*, 46 (1971) pp. 477–90.

17. W. M. Ormrod, 'Edward III and his Family', *JBS*, 26 (1987) pp. 398–422; C. Allmand, *Henry V* (London: Methuen, 1992) pp. 333–48.

18. R. A. Griffiths, *King and Country: England and Wales in the Fifteenth Century* (London: Hambledon Press, 1991) pp. 89–92.

19. Given-Wilson (ed.), *Chronicles of the Revolution*, pp. 74–5.

20. G. Holmes, *The Good Parliament* (Oxford: Clarendon Press, 1975) p. 156; Griffiths, *King and Country*, pp. 3–4.

21. For what follows, see C. Given-Wilson, *The Royal Household and the King's Affinity* (London and New Haven: Yale University Press, 1986) pp. 110–41; B. P. Wolffe, 'Acts of Resumption in the Lancastrian Parliaments', in E. B. Fryde and E. Miller (eds), *Historical Studies of the English Parliament* (Cambridge: Cambridge University Press, 1970) vol. 2, pp. 61–91; W.M. Ormrod, 'The Politics of Pestilence: Government in England after the Black Death' (forthcoming).

22. A. Rogers, 'Henry IV, the Commons and Taxation', *Mediaeval Studies*, 31 (1969) pp. 44–70; G. L. Harriss, 'Theory and Practice in Royal Taxation', *EHR*, 97 (1982) pp. 811–19; A. Rogers, 'Clerical Taxation under Henry IV', *BIHR*, 46 (1973) pp. 123–44.

23. For what follows, see J. Dunbabin, 'Government', in J. H. Burns (ed.),

The Cambridge History of Medieval Political Thought (Cambridge: Cambridge University Press, 1988) pp. 477–519.

24. *EHD*, 3, p. 525; H. G. Richardson, 'The English Coronation Oath', *Speculum*, 24 (1949) pp. 44–75.

25. M. McKisack, *The Fourteenth Century* (Oxford: Clarendon Press, 1959) pp. 5–6; D. Clementi, 'That the Statute of York of 1322 is No Longer Ambiguous', in *Album Helen Maud Cam*, Studies Presented to the International Commission for the History of Representative and Parliamentary Institutions 23–4 (Louvain, 1960–1) vol. 2, pp. 93–100; W. M. Ormrod, 'Edward III and the Recovery of Royal Authority in England', *History*, 72 (1987) pp. 11–12; S. B. Chrimes, 'Richard II's Questions to the Judges, 1387', *Law Quarterly Review*, 72 (1956) pp. 365–90.

26. Given-Wilson (ed.), *Chronicles of the Revolution*, pp. 177–8.

27. B. Wilkinson, *Constitutional History of England in the Fifteenth Century* (London: Longman, 1964) pp. 42–3.

28. S. J. Payling, 'The Ampthill Dispute', *EHR*, 104 (1989) pp. 881–907.

29. W. M. Ormrod, *The Reign of Edward III* (London and New Haven: Yale University Press, 1990) pp. 55–6; G. L. Harriss, 'The King and his Magnates', in Harriss (ed.), *Henry V*, pp. 46–7.

30. R. L. Storey, *The End of the House of Lancaster*, rev. edn (Gloucester: Alan Sutton, 1986) esp. p. 27.

31. For what follows, see Dunbabin, 'Government', p. 492; J. G. Bellamy, *The Law of Treason in England in the Middle Ages* (Cambridge: Cambridge University Press, 1970).

32. Given-Wilson (ed.), *Chronicles of the Revolution*, pp. 180–1.

33. For the contrary view, see W. H. Dunham and C. T. Wood, 'The Right to Rule in England', *American Historical Review*, 81 (1976) pp. 738–61; and, for a rebuff, J. W. McKenna, 'The Myth of Parliamentary Sovereignty in late Medieval England', *EHR*, 94 (1979) pp. 481–506.

34. S. B. Chrimes and A. L. Brown (eds), *Select Documents of English Constitutional History 1307–1485* (London: A. & C. Black, 1961) p. 5; Dunbabin, 'Government', pp. 500–1. For the citation of the 1308 protestation in 1321, see N. Pronay and J. Taylor (eds), *Parliamentary Texts of the Later Middle Ages* (Oxford: Clarendon Press, 1980) pp. 156–9.

35. Chrimes and Brown (eds), *Select Documents*, pp. 37–8; W. Stubbs, *The Constitutional History of England*, 4th edn (Oxford: Clarendon Press, 1906) vol. 3, pp. 383–4; E. M. Peters, *The Shadow King* (London and New Haven: Yale University Press, 1970).

36. See A. Tuck, *Crown and Nobility 1272–1461* (London: Fontana, 1985) p. 93, with references. For the (unlikely) possibility of Edward II's escape, see G. P. Cuttino and T. W. Lyman, 'Where is Edward II?', *Speculum*, 53 (1978) pp. 522–44.

37. M. V. Clarke, *Medieval Representation and Consent* (London: Longman, 1936) pp. 173–95.

38. *EHD*, 4, pp. 72–3; J. R. Lumby (ed.), *Chronicon Henrici Knighton*, Rolls Series 92 (London, 1889–95) vol. 2, p. 219.

39. M. V. Clarke, *Fourteenth Century Studies* (Oxford: Clarendon Press, 1937) pp. 91–5.

40. In addition to the attempted canonisation of Edward II, see the neglected parliamentary declaration of 1391 (T. F. Tout, *Chapters in the Administrative History of Mediaeval England* (Manchester: Manchester University Press, 1920–33) vol. 3, p. 474) that provides the context for article 17 of the deposition articles (Given-Wilson (ed.), *Chronicles of the Revolution*, p. 178).

41. Tuck, *Crown and Nobility*, p. 219, with references.

42. C. Ross, *Edward IV* (London: Methuen, 1974) pp. 27–38.

43. P. S. Lewis, 'Two Pieces of Fifteenth-century Political Iconography', *Journal of the Warburg and Courtauld Institutes*, 27 (1964) pp. 319–20; R. H. Robbins (ed.), *Historical Poems of the XIVth and XVth Centuries* (New York: Columbia University Press, 1959), pp. 174–5.

44. C. Richmond, 'The Nobility and the Wars of the Roses', *Nottingham Medieval Studies*, 21 (1977) pp. 71–85.

5 POLITICAL ISSUES: WAR

1. The classic statement, employing this terminology, is R. W. Kaeuper, *War, Justice and Public Order* (Oxford: Clarendon Press, 1988).

2. J. B. Gillingham, 'Crisis or Continuity? The Structure of Royal Authority in England, 1360–1422', *Vorträge und Forschungen*, 32 (1987) pp. 59–80; G. L. Harriss, 'Political Society and the Growth of Government in Late Medieval England', *P&P*, 138 (1993) pp. 28–57; W. M. Ormrod, ' The Politics of Pestilence: Government in England after the Black Death' (forthcoming).

3. J. R. Maddicott, 'Magna Carta and the Local Community, 1215–1259', *P&P*, 102 (1984) pp. 25–65; J. S. Illsley, 'The Medieval Gentry and the English Constitution', *Medieval History*, 3 (1993) pp. 3–20.

4. R. C. Palmer, *English Law in the Age of the Black Death* (Chapel Hill, NC: University of North Carolina Press, 1993) pp. 1–56.

5. The following two paragraphs depend principally on M. R. Powicke, *Military Obligation in Medieval England* (Oxford: Clarendon Press, 1962).

6. W. R. Jones, 'Purveyance for War and the Community of the Realm', *Albion*, 7 (1975) pp. 300–16.

7. For what follows, see in particular P. Morgan, *War and Society in Medieval Cheshire 1277–1403*, Chetham Soc. 3rd series 34 (Manchester, 1987); A.

Curry, 'The First English Standing Army?', in C. Ross (ed.), *Patronage, Pedigree and Power in Later Medieval England* (Gloucester: Alan Sutton, 1979) pp. 193–214; M. H. Keen, 'English Military Experience and the Court of Chivalry: the Case of Grey v. Hastings', in P. Contamine, C. Giry-Deloison and M. H. Keen (eds), *Guerre et société en France, en Angleterre et en Bourgogne xive–xve siècle* (Lille: Université Charles de Gaulle, 1991) pp. 123–42.

8. M. Keen, 'The End of the Hundred Years War', in M. Jones and M. Vale (eds), *England and her Neighbours 1066–1453* (London: Hambledon Press, 1989) pp. 297–311 and the sources cited there.

9. This calculation and much of what follows is based on the statistical material discussed in W. M. Ormrod, 'The Crown and the English Economy 1290–1348', in B. M. S. Campbell (ed.), *Before the Black Death* (Manchester: Manchester University Press, 1991) pp. 149–83; W. M. Ormrod, 'The Domestic Response to the Hundred Years War', in A. Curry and M. Hughes (eds), *Arms, Armies and Fortifications in the Hundred Years War* (Woodbridge: Boydell Press, 1994) pp. 87–94; W. M. Ormrod, 'England in the Middle Ages', in R. Bonney (ed.), *The Rise of the Fiscal State in Europe 1200–1800* (forthcoming).

10. J. R. Maddicott, 'Poems of Social Protest in Early Fourteenth Century England', in W. M. Ormrod (ed.), *England in the Fourteenth Century* (Woodbridge: Boydell Press, 1986) p. 132; H. Barr (ed.), *The Piers Plowman Tradition* (London: Dent, 1993) p. 206.

11. E. M. Carus-Wilson and O. Coleman, *England's Export Trade, 1275–1547* (Oxford: Clarendon Press, 1963) pp. 22–3.

12. Ormrod, 'Domestic Response', p. 94 and n. 16.

13. J. R. Maddicott, 'The English Peasantry and the Demands of the Crown, 1294–1341', in T. H. Aston (ed.), *Landlords, Peasants and Politics in Medieval England* (Cambridge: Cambridge University Press, 1987) pp. 285–359.

14. For what follows, see M. Prestwich, 'England and Scotland during the Wars of Independence', in Jones and Vale (eds), *England and her Neighbours*, pp. 181–97.

15. G. L. Harriss, *King, Parliament and Public Finance in Medieval England to 1369* (Oxford: Clarendon Press, 1975) pp. 92–7, 348–54, 383–400; N. B. Lewis, 'The Last Summons of the English Feudal Levy', *EHR*, 73 (1958) pp. 1–26; N. B. Lewis, 'The Feudal Summons of 1385', *EHR*, 100 (1985) pp. 729–43. It is significant, as Lewis notes, that the circumstances in 1385 implied as much a French as a Scottish invasion.

16. J. Le Patourel, *Feudal Empires* (London: Hambledon Press, 1984) ch. VIII; M. G. A. Vale, 'The Gascon Nobility and the Anglo-French War, 1294–98', in J. C. Holt and J. Gillingham (eds), *War and Government in the*

Middle Ages (Woodbridge: Boydell Press, 1984) pp. 136–7; Harriss, *King, Parliament*, pp. 34–8, 41–4, 49–52.

17. For the methods used to recruit the armies of Flanders in 1297 and 1338–40, see N. B. Lewis, 'The English Forces in Flanders, August-November 1297', in R. W. Hunt, W. A. Pantin and R. W. Southern (eds), *Studies in Medieval History Presented to F. M. Powicke* (Oxford: Clarendon Press, 1948) pp. 310–18; M. Prestwich, 'English Armies in the Early Stages of the Hundred Years War', *BIHR*, 56 (1983) pp. 102–13.

18. For Edward I's faltering use of the plea of necessity see M. Prestwich (ed.), *Documents Illustrating the Crisis of 1297–8 in England*, Camden Soc. 4th series 24 (London, 1980) pp. 28–30.

19. Harriss, *King, Parliament*, pp. 314–20.

20. A. Grant, *Independence and Nationhood* (London: Edward Arnold, 1984) pp. 55–7. For the failure of the English crown to make dynastic capital out of the capture of David II and James I, see W. M. Ormrod, 'Edward III and his Family', *JBS*, 26 (1987) pp. 409–11; P. J. Bradley, 'Henry V's Scottish Policy', in J. S. Hamilton and P. J. Bradley (eds), *Documenting the Past* (Woodbridge: Boydell Press, 1989) pp. 177–95.

21. For disillusionment in the 1360s see J. Barnie, *War in Medieval Society* (London: Weidenfeld and Nicolson, 1974) pp. 13–14.

22. L. C. Hector and B. F. Harvey (eds), *The Westminster Chronicle 1381–1394* (Oxford: Clarendon Press, 1982) pp. 516–18, cited and discussed by A. Tuck, 'Richard II and the Hundred Years War', in J. Taylor and W. Childs (eds), *Politics and Crisis in Fourteenth Century England* (Gloucester: Alan Sutton, 1990) pp. 126–7.

23. G. L. Harriss, 'The Management of Parliament', in G. L. Harriss (ed.), *Henry V: The Practice of Kingship* (Oxford: Oxford University Press, 1985) pp. 146–9.

24. J. A. Tuck, 'The Emergence of a Northern Nobility, 1250–1400', *Northern History*, 22 (1986) pp. 1–17.

25. K. B. McFarlane, *The Nobility of Later Medieval England* (Oxford: Clarendon Press, 1973) pp. 19–40; A. J. Pollard, *John Talbot and the War in France* (London: Royal Historical Society, 1983) p. 120; Keen, 'End of the Hundred Years War', pp. 304–5.

26. See, e.g., S. Walker, 'Profit and Loss in the Hundred Years War', *BIHR*, 58 (1985) pp. 100–6; A. Ayton, 'War and the English Gentry under Edward III', *History Today*, 42, no. 5 (1992) pp. 34–40.

27. J. M. W. Bean, 'Henry IV and the Percies', *History*, 44 (1959) pp. 212–27; J. M. W. Bean, 'The Financial Position of Richard, Duke of York', in Holt and Gillingham (eds), *War and Government*, pp. 182–98.

28. A. Goodman, *The Loyal Conspiracy* (London: Routledge & Kegan Paul, 1971) pp. 124–6; M. K. Jones, 'John Beaufort, Duke of Somerset, and

the French Expedition of 1443', in R. A. Griffiths (ed.), *Patronage, the Crown and the Provinces in Later Medieval England* (Gloucester: Alan Sutton, 1981) pp. 75–102.

29. P. S. Lewis, 'War Propaganda and Historiography in Fifteenth-century France and England', *TRHS*, 4th series 15 (1965) p. 8; Keen, 'End of the Hundred Years War', p. 298.

30. For what follows, see E. B. Fryde, *Studies in Medieval Trade and Finance* (London: Hambledon Press, 1983) esp. chapters VI, X; T. H. Lloyd, *The English Wool Trade in the Middle Ages* (Cambridge: Cambridge University Press, 1977).

31. J. L. Kirby, 'The Financing of Calais under Henry V', *BIHR*, 50 (1923) pp. 165–77.

32. G. L. Harriss, 'The Struggle for Calais: an Aspect of the Rivalry between Lancaster and York', *EHR*, 75 (1960) pp. 30–53.

33. G. A. Holmes, 'The "Libel of English Policy"', *EHR*, 76 (1961) pp. 193–216.

34. Maddicott, 'English Peasantry', pp. 329–51; Ormrod, 'The Crown and the English Economy', pp. 181–3.

35. R. H. Hilton, *Class Conflict and the Crisis of Feudalism*, 2nd edn (London: Verso, 1990) pp. 12–18, 49–65; R. H. Hilton, 'Resistance to Taxation and to other State Impositions in Medieval England', in J.-P. Genet and M. le Mené (eds), *Genèse de l'état moderne: prélèvement et redistribution* (Paris: Éditions du CNRS, 1987) pp. 171–5.

36. E. Searle and R. Burghart, 'The Defense of England and the Peasants' Revolt', *Viator*, 3 (1972) pp. 365–88.

37. Ormrod, 'Politics of Pestilence'.

38. P. McNiven, 'The Betrayal of Archbishop Scrope', *Bulletin of the John Rylands Library*, 54 (1971–2) pp. 173–213, esp. pp. 181–3.

39. R. L. Virgoe, 'The Death of William de la Pole', *Bulletin of the John Rylands Library*, 47 (1964–5) pp. 489–502.

6 POLITICAL ISSUES: JUSTICE

1. E. Powell, 'After "After McFarlane"', in D. J. Clayton, R. G. Davies and P. McNiven (eds), *Trade, Devotion and Governance* (Stroud: Alan Sutton, 1994) pp. 1–16.

2. E. Powell, *Kingship, Law, and Society* (Oxford: Clarendon Press, 1989) pp. 9–12, with references.

3. B. W. McLane, 'Changes in the Court of King's Bench, 1291–1340', in W. M. Ormrod (ed.), *England in the Fourteenth Century* (Woodbridge: Boydell Press, 1986) pp. 158–9. See also R. W. Kaeuper, 'Law and Order in Fourteenth-century England: the Evidence of Special Commissions of Oyer and Terminer', *Speculum*, 54 (1979) pp. 747–53.

4. R. C. Palmer, *English Law in the Age of the Black Death* (Chapel Hill, NC: University of North Carolina Press, 1993) pp. 169–293.

5. N. Saul, 'Conflict and Consensus in English Local Society', in J. Taylor and W. Childs (eds), *Politics and Crisis in Fourteenth-Century England* (Gloucester: Alan Sutton, 1990) p. 42.

6. As argued by K. B. McFarlane, *The Nobility of Later Medieval England* (Oxford: Clarendon Press, 1973) pp. 115–18; G. L. Harriss, 'Introduction', in K. B. McFarlane, *England in the Fifteenth Century*, (London: Hambledon Press, 1981) pp. xix–xx.

7. For what follows, see D. Crook, 'The Later Eyres', *EHR*, 117 (1982) pp. 241–68.

8. A. Verduyn, 'The Politics of Law and Order during the Early Years of Edward III', *EHR*, 108 (1993) pp. 842–67.

9. A. Harding, 'The Origins and Early History of the Keeper of the Peace', *TRHS*, 5th series 10 (1960) pp. 85–109; B. H. Putnam, 'The Transformation of the Keepers of the Peace into the Justices of the Peace', *TRHS*, 4th series 12 (1929) pp. 19–48.

10. E. Powell, 'The Administration of Criminal Justice in Late-medieval England', in R. Eales and D. Sullivan (eds), *The Political Context of Law* (London: Hambledon Press, 1987) pp. 53–5, with references.

11. See the summary of recent writing on this theme in G. L. Harriss, 'Political Society and the Growth of Government in Late Medieval England', *P&P*, 138 (1993) pp. 28–30. For the long view, M. L. Bush, *The English Aristocracy* (Manchester: Manchester University Press, 1984) p. 198.

12. A. J. Verduyn, 'The Attitude of the Parliamentary Commons to Law and Order under Edward III', University of Oxford D.Phil. thesis (1991) pp. 1–106.

13. A. J. Musson, 'Public Order and Law Enforcement in England 1294–1350', University of Cambridge Ph.D. thesis (1993) pp. 8–168, 228–39.

14. Powell, 'Administration of Criminal Justice', pp. 49–59. See also S. Walker, 'Yorkshire Justices of the Peace, 1389–1413', *EHR*, 108 (1993) pp. 281–311.

15. Powell, *Kingship, Law, and Society*, pp. 19–20; Palmer, *English Law*, pp. 14–27.

16. E. B. Fryde and N. Fryde, 'Peasant Rebellion and Peasant Discontents', in E. Miller (ed.), *The Agrarian History of England and Wales, III: 1348–1500* (Cambridge: Cambridge University Press, 1991) pp. 753–60.

17. W. M. Ormrod, *The Reign of Edward III* (London and New Haven: Yale University Press, 1990) p. 147; R. Faith, 'The "Great Rumour" of 1377 and Peasant Ideology', in R. H. Hilton and T. H. Aston (eds), *The English Rising of 1381* (Cambridge: Cambridge University Press, 1984), pp. 43–7.

18. A. Harding, 'The Revolt against the Justices', in Hilton and Aston (eds), *The English Rising of 1381*, pp. 165–93.

19. J. R. Maddicott, 'Poems of Social Protest in Early Fourteenth Century England', in Ormrod (ed.), *England in the Fourteenth Century*, pp. 138–9; for further examples of the use of this phrase, see R. F. Green, 'John Ball's Letters', in B. A. Hanawalt (ed.) *Chaucer's England* (Minneapolis: University of Minnesota Press, 1992) pp. 183–4.

20. Harding, 'Revolt against the Justices', pp. 178–80; N. Brooks, 'The Organization and Achievements of the Peasants of Kent and Essex in 1381', in H. Mayr-Harting and R. I. Moore (eds), *Studies in Medieval History Presented to R. H. C. Davies* (London: Hambledon Press, 1985) pp. 247–70; W. M. Ormrod, 'The Peasants' Revolt and the Government of England', *JBS*, 29 (1990) pp. 2–19.

21. Powell, 'Administration of Criminal Justice', pp. 54–5, and the sources cited there.

22. S. A. C. Penn and C. Dyer, 'Wages and Earnings in Late Medieval England', *Economic History Review*, 2nd series 43 (1990) pp. 356–76.

23. R. B. Dobson (ed.), *The Peasants' Revolt of 1381*, 2nd edn (London: Macmillan, 1983) p. 339.

24. R. H. Robbins (ed.), *Historical Poems of the XIVth and XVth Centuries* (New York: Columbia University Press, 1959) pp. 130–4.

25. L. R. Poos, 'The Social Context of Statute of Labourers Enforcement', *Law and History Review*, 1 (1983) pp. 27–52.

26. J. G. Bellamy, *Crime and Public Order in England in the Later Middle Ages* (London: Routledge & Kegan Paul, 1973) pp. 34–5; J. B. Post, 'Some Limitations of the Medieval Peace Rolls', *Journal of the Society of Archivists*, 4 (1973) pp. 633–9; R. H. Hilton, *The English Peasantry in the Late Middle Ages* (Oxford: Clarendon Press, 1975) pp. 51–3.

27. Dobson (ed.), *Peasants' Revolt*, pp. 340–1.

28. Powell, *Kingship, Law, and Society*, pp. 112–14.

29. C. Carpenter, 'Law, Justice and Landowners in Late Medieval England', *Law and History Review*, 1 (1983) pp. 225–31; W. M. Ormrod, 'Agenda for Legislation, 1322–c. 1340', *EHR*, 105 (1990) pp. 19–22; J. R. Maddicott, *Law and Lordship*, *P&P* Supplement 4 (Cambridge, 1978) pp. 60–71; R. L. Storey, *The End of House of Lancaster*, rev. edn (Gloucester: Alan Sutton, 1986) p. 26; J. L. Watts, 'Domestic Politics and the Constitution in the Reign of Henry VI, c. 1435–61', University of Cambridge Ph.D. thesis (1990) pp. 67–8; C. Carpenter, *Locality and Polity* (Cambridge: Cambridge University Press, 1992) pp. 1–10.

30. For what follows, see J. A. Tuck, 'The Cambridge Parliament 1388', *EHR*, 74 (1969) pp. 225–43; R. L. Storey, 'Liveries and Commissions of

the Peace 1388–90', in F. R. H. Du Boulay and C. M. Barron (eds), *The Reign of Richard II* (London: Athlone Press, 1971) pp. 131–52; P. Strohm, *Hochon's Arrow* (Princeton, NJ: Princeton University Press, 1992) pp. 57–74.

31. For what follows, see Maddicott, *Law and Lordship*, pp. 71–81.

32. J. M. W. Bean, *From Lord to Patron* (Manchester: Manchester University Press, 1989) pp. 203–5; C. Given-Wilson, *The Royal Household and the King's Affinity* (London and New Haven: Yale University Press, 1986) pp. 250–1.

33. Bean, *Lord to Patron*, pp. 205–11; N. Saul, 'The Commons and the Abolition of Badges', *Parliamentary History*, 9 (1990) pp. 302–5.

34. N. Saul, *Knights and Esquires* (Oxford: Clarendon Press, 1981) pp. 110–11.

35. See above, chapter 3, at n. 26. For the numerical importance of the lawyers on the peace commissions in the first half of the fifteenth century, see Carpenter, *Locality and Polity*, pp. 267–72.

36. S. M. Wright, *The Derbyshire Gentry in the Fifteenth Century*, Derbyshire Record Society 8 (Chesterfield, 1983) p. 94; S. Payling, *Political Society in Lancastrian England* (Oxford: Clarendon Press, 1991) p. 178.

37. See the language used by Palmer, *English Law*, pp. 1–7, 57, 137.

38. A. Herbert, 'Herefordshire: Some Aspects of Society and Public Order', in R. A. Griffiths (ed.), *Patronage, the Crown and the Provinces in Later Medieval England* (Gloucester: Alan Sutton, 1981) pp. 105–6; Griffiths, *Reign of King Henry VI*, p. 136.

39. P. C. Maddern, *Violence and Social Order* (Oxford: Clarendon Press, 1992) pp. 206–25.

40. Griffiths, *Reign of King Henry VI*, pp. 584–8.

41. N. D. Hurnard, *The King's Pardon for Homicide before 1307* (Oxford: Clarendon Press, 1969) pp. 311–26; H. J. Hewitt, *The Organization of War under Edward III* (Manchester: Manchester University Press, 1966) pp. 29–31, 173–5.

42. E. L. G. Stones, 'The Folvilles of Ashby Folville', *TRHS*, 5th series 7 (1957) pp. 117–36; see also J. G. Bellamy, 'The Coterel Gang', *EHR*, 79 (1964) pp. 698–717.

43. Maddicott, 'Poems of Social Protest', p. 132; R. W. Kaeuper, 'An Historian's Reading of *The Tale of Gamelyn*', *Medium Aevum*, 52 (1983) pp. 51–62; J. R. Maddicott, 'The Birth and Settings of the Ballads of Robin Hood', *EHR*, 93 (1978) pp. 276–99; but see also J. C. Holt, *Robin Hood* (London: Thames & Hudson, 1982) pp. 59–60.

44. Powell, *Kingship, Law, and Society*, pp. 233–6; Bellamy, *Crime and Public Order*, pp. 83–4.

45. For a more cynical view of Edward's real record, see J. Aberth, 'Crime and Justice under Edward III', *EHR*, 107 (1992) pp. 283–301.
46. For what follows, see E. Powell, 'The Restoration of Law and Order', in G. L. Harriss (ed.), *Henry V: The Practice of Kingship* (Oxford: Oxford University Press, 1985) pp. 53–74.
47. Griffiths, *Reign of King Henry VI*, pp. 588–92.
48. Harriss, 'Introduction', in McFarlane, *Fifteenth Century*, pp. xix–xx; M. T. Clanchy, 'Law, Government and Society in Medieval England', *History* 59 (1974) pp. 73–8.

7 POLITICAL LIFE

1. V. J. Scattergood, *Politics and Poetry in the Fifteenth Century* (London: Blandford Press, 1971) pp. 264–349.
2. G. Bois, *The Crisis of Feudalism* (Cambridge: Cambridge University Press, 1984); W. M. Ormrod, 'The West European Monarchies in the later Middle Ages', in R. Bonney (ed.), *Economic Systems and State Finance* (Oxford: Oxford University Press, 1995).
3. C. Plummer (ed.), *The Governance of England* (Oxford: Clarendon Press, 1885) p. 109.
4. Scattergood, *Politics and Poetry*, p. 284.
5. A. L. Brown, 'The Commons and the Council in the Reign of Henry IV', in E. B. Fryde and E. Miller (eds), *Historical Studies of the English Parliament* (Cambridge: Cambridge University Press, 1970) vol. 2, p. 43.
6. J. L. Watts, 'Domestic Politics and the Constitution in the Reign of Henry VI, *c.* 1435–61', University of Cambridge Ph.D. thesis (1990) pp. 67–8.
7. K. B. McFarlane, *England in the Fifteenth Century* (London: Hambledon Press, 1981) pp. 42, 238–9.
8. G. L. Harriss, 'The Formation of Parliament', in R. G. Davies and J. H. Denton (eds), *The English Parliament in the Middle Ages* (Manchester: Manchester University Press, 1981) pp. 45–7.
9. W. M. Ormrod, 'England in the Middle Ages', in R. Bonney (ed.), *The Rise of the Fiscal State in Europe 1200–1800* (forthcoming) with references.
10. Though see M. K. Jones, 'Somerset, York and the Wars of the Roses', *EHR*, 104 (1989) pp. 285–307.
11. Thus I extend the theme of the 'tragic dilemma' propounded by A. R. Myers, *England in the Later Middle Ages* (Harmondsworth: Penguin Books, 1971) pp. 15–36.

BIBLIOGRAPHY

This bibliography is a short selection of major books and collections of essays relevant to fourteenth- and early fifteenth-century politics. Specialised articles and monographs are deliberately excluded, though at least some of them may be located via the preceding notes. Fuller bibliographies may be found in the Royal Historical Society's annual *Bibliography of British and Irish History*.

Allmand, C., *Henry V* (London: Methuen, 1992). Important new biography.

Barnie, J., *War in Medieval Society: Social Values and the Hundred Years War, 1337–99* (London: Weidenfeld and Nicolson, 1974). The domestic response to war.

Bennett, M. J., *Community, Class and Careerism: Cheshire and Lancashire Society in the Age of* Sir Gawain and the Green Knight (Cambridge: Cambridge University Press, 1983). Sophisticated approach taking in cultural, as well as political, history.

Brown, A. L., *The Governance of Late Medieval England 1272–1461* (London: Edward Arnold, 1989). Conventional summary of the structure of administration and justice; good too on parliament.

Carpenter, C., *Locality and Polity: A Study of Warwickshire Landed Society, 1401–1499* (Cambridge: Cambridge University Press, 1992). Fuller and more wide-ranging than most of the other county studies: many important issues and ideas.

Chrimes, S. B., Ross C. D. and Griffiths, R. A. (eds), *Fifteenth-Century England*

(Manchester: Manchester University Press, 1972). Now slightly old-fashioned, but several seminal contributions.

Curry, A., *The Hundred Years War* (Basingstoke: Macmillan, 1993). Best recent study of the diplomacy of war.

Davies, R. G. and Denton, J. H. (eds), *The English Parliament in the Middle Ages* (Manchester: Manchester University Press, 1981). Important contributions by Harriss, Maddicott, Brown and Myers.

Du Boulay, F. R. H. and Barron, C. M. (eds), *The Reign of Richard II* (London: Athlone Press, 1971). Lively and influential collection.

Dyer, C., *Standards of Living in the Later Middle Ages* (Cambridge: Cambridge University Press, 1989). The economic and social context.

Frame, R., *The Political Development of the British Isles 1100–1400* (Oxford: Oxford University Press, 1990). English politics in a wider context.

Fryde, N., *The Tyranny and Fall of Edward II 1321–1326* (Cambridge: Cambridge University Press, 1979). The rule of the Despensers.

Given-Wilson, C., *The Royal Household and the King's Affinity: Service, Politics and Finance in England 1360–1413* (London and New Haven: Yale University Press, 1986). Important study of the rise of the royal affinity.

Given-Wilson, C., *The English Nobility in the Late Middle Ages* (London: Routledge & Kegan Paul, 1987). Summarises recent research and includes the gentry.

Goodman, A., *John of Gaunt* (Harlow: Longman, 1992). Sets Gaunt in his international, as well as his English, political role.

Green, R. F., *Poets and Princepleasers* (Toronto: University of Toronto Press, 1980). The cultural and political context of the court.

Griffiths, R. A., *The Reign of King Henry VI* (London: Ernest Benn, 1981). Daunting dimensions, but a rich source of ideas and material.

Hanawalt, B. A., *Crime and Conflict in English Communities, 1300–1348* (Cambridge, Mass.: Harvard University Press, 1979). Controversial but interesting study of lawlessness.

Harriss, G. L. (ed.), *Henry V: The Practice of Kingship* (Oxford: Oxford University Press, 1985). Ideal introduction to this most challenging of kings.

Harvey, I. M. W., *Jack Cade's Rebellion of 1450* (Oxford: Clarendon Press, 1991). New and definitive study.

Heath, P., *Church and Realm 1272–1461* (London: Fontana, 1988). The church in politics.

Hilton, R. H., *Bond Men Made Free* (London: Methuen, 1977). Hilton's personal assessment of 1381.

Hilton, R. H. and Aston, T. H. (eds), *The English Rising of 1381* (Cambridge: Cambridge University Press, 1984). Includes several highly influential studies of the Peasants' Revolt.

Johnson, P. A., *Duke Richard of York 1411–1460* (Oxford: Clarendon Press, 1988). Relentless narrative, but full of information.

Kaeuper, R. W., *War, Justice, and Public Order: England and France in the Later Middle Ages* (Oxford: Clarendon Press, 1988). Major comparative study of the shift from law state to war state.

Keen, M. H., *England in the Later Middle Ages* (London: Methuen, 1973). Still the most popular textbook for the high politics of the period.

Keen, M. H., *English Society in the Later Middle Ages 1348–1500* (London: Allen Lane, 1990). Useful summary of social and political change.

Lander, J. R., *The Limitations of English Monarchy in the Later Middle Ages* (Toronto: University of Toronto Press, 1989). Vigorous and in places controversial essay; full bibliography of Lander's work.

McFarlane, K. B., *The Nobility of Later Medieval England* (Oxford: Clarendon Press, 1973). Revised by more recent work, but a classic statement.

McFarlane, K. B., *England in the Fifteenth Century* (London: Hambledon Press, 1981). Includes McFarlane's essays on bastard feudalism and the Wars of the Roses.

Maddern, P. C., *Violence and Social Order: East Anglia 1422–1442* (Oxford: Clarendon Press, 1992). Subtle and sophisticated new study of the meaning of violence.

Maddicott, J. R., *Thomas of Lancaster* (Oxford: Clarendon Press, 1970). Major political biography: the best study of Edward II's reign.

Mertes, K., *The English Noble Household 1250–1600* (Oxford: Basil Blackwell, 1988). Essential for an understanding of 'domestic' politics.

Ormrod, W. M., *The Reign of Edward III: Crown and Political Society in England 1327–1377* (London and New Haven: Yale University Press, 1990). Up-beat – some would say optimistic – interpretation of the reign.

Payling, S., *Political Society in Lancastrian England: The Major Gentry of Nottinghamshire* (Oxford: Clarendon Press, 1991). A 'horizontal' polity.

Powell, E., *Kingship, Law, and Society: Criminal Justice in the Reign of Henry V* (Oxford: Clarendon Press, 1989). Ranges widely; best study of the meaning of justice in this period.

Prestwich, M., *The Three Edwards* (London: Weidenfeld and Nicolson, 1980). Vigorous, readable study of war and the state.

Prestwich, M., *Edward I* (London: Methuen, 1988). A major, and definitive, biography.

Reynolds, S., *An Introduction to the History of English Medieval Towns* (Oxford: Clarendon Press, 1977). Good survey of urban constitutional history.

Saul, N., *Knights and Esquires: The Gloucestershire Gentry in the Fourteenth Century* (Oxford: Clarendon Press, 1981). Ground-breaking study of local political society.

Storey, R. L., *The End of the House of Lancaster,* rev. edn (Gloucester: Alan Sutton, 1986). Bastard feudalism and the Wars of the Roses.

Thomson, J. A. F., *The Transformation of Medieval England 1370–1529* (Harlow: Longman, 1983). Chronology and analysis.

Tuck, A., *Richard II and the English Nobility* (London: Edward Arnold, 1973). The best study of Richard's reign currently available.

Tuck, A., *Crown and Nobility 1272–1461* (London: Fontana, 1985). Good textbook of high politics.

Vale, J., *Edward III and Chivalry: Chivalric Society and its Context 1270–1350* (Woodbridge: Boydell Press, 1982). Especially important for the Order of the Garter.

Walker, S., *The Lancastrian Affinity 1361–1399* (Oxford: Clarendon Press, 1990). Bastard feudalism re-assessed.

Waugh, S. L., *England in the Reign of Edward III* (Cambridge: Cambridge University Press, 1991). Wide-ranging study which, despite its title, takes in much of the period 1272–1377.

Wolffe, B., *Henry VI* (London: Methuen, 1981). Controversial study which sees Henry as actively responsible for his own government.

INDEX

162